D1100807

31BC
ANTONY, CLEOPATRA AND THE FALL OF
EGYPT

31BC

ANTONY, CLEOPATRA AND THE FALL OF

EGYPT

DAVID STUTTARD & SAM MOORHEAD

THE BRITISH MUSEUM PRESS

© 2012 The Trustees of the British Museum

First published in 2012 by The British Museum Press
A division of The British Museum Company Ltd
38 Russell Square
London WC1B 3QQ
britishmuseum.org/publishing

A catalogue record for this book is available from the
British Library

ISBN: 978-0-7141-2274-8

Designed by Bobby Birchall, Bobby and Co.
Printed in Hong Kong by Printing Express Company Ltd

The papers used by the British Museum are recyclable
products and the manufacturing processes are expected
to conform to the environmental regulations of the
country of origin.

The majority of objects illustrated in this book are from
the collection of the British Museum and are © The
Trustees of the British Museum. The British Museum
registration numbers for these objects are listed in the
corresponding captions. You can find out more about
objects in all areas of the British Museum collection
on the Museum's website at britishmuseum.org/
research/search_the_collection_database.aspx

Frontispiece Antony taking leave of Cleopatra by
Francis Philip Stephanoff (1789–1860).
Watercolour and bodycolour, Britain, *c.*1838–45.
24.8 x 19.7 cm. British Museum, 1977,1105.6.

Contents

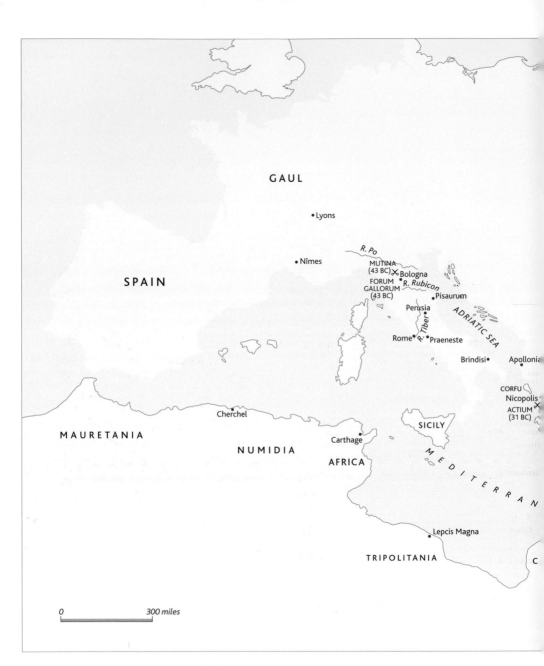

GAUL

• Lyons

R. Po

• Nîmes

SPAIN

MUTINA
(43 BC) ✕ • Bologna
FORUM   R. *Rubicon*
GALLORUM
(43 BC)   • Pisaurum

Perusia   ADRIATIC SEA

R. *Tiber*

Rome • • Praeneste

Brindisi •   • Apollonia

CORFU
Nicopolis
ACTIUM ✕
(31 BC)

Cherchel •

MAURETANIA   SICILY

NUMIDIA

Carthage •

AFRICA   M E D I T E R R A N

Lepcis Magna •

TRIPOLITANIA   C

0   300 miles

The Roman Empire in the late
Republican period, *c.*50–31 BC.

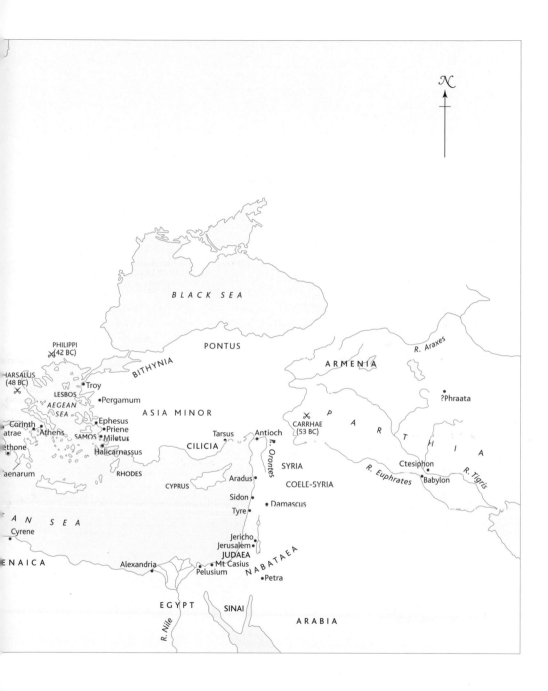

BLACK SEA

PONTUS

R. Araxes

ARMENIA

?Phraata

PHILIPPI
(42 BC)

BITHYNIA

HARSALUS
(48 BC)

Troy

LESBOS

Pergamum

AEGEAN
SEA

ASIA MINOR

CARRHAE
(53 BC)

P
A
R
T
H
I
A

Corinth
atrae

Ephesus
Priene
Athens
SAMOS Miletus

Tarsus

Antioch

ethone

CILICIA

Orontes

R. Euphrates

Ctesiphon

R. Tigris

Halicarnassus

SYRIA

Babylon

aenarum

RHODES

CYPRUS

Aradus

COELE-SYRIA

Sidon

Damascus

A   N   SEA

Tyre

Cyrene

Jericho

ENAICA

Jerusalem

JUDAEA

N
A
B
A
T
A
E
A

Alexandria

Mt Casius

Pelusium

Petra

EGYPT

SINAI

ARABIA

R. Nile

Timeline

Introduction

ON 2 SEPTEMBER 31 BC, two superpowers met head-on for the first and last time in history: the mythically ancient, mystically religious civilization of Egypt and the pragmatic, efficient, newly brutalized military regime of Rome. The outcome of the Battle of Actium was to change the course of history and lead to the foundation of the Roman Empire.

Among the prizes which went to the winner, Octavian (soon-to-be emperor Augustus), and his staff of what today would be called spin-doctors, was the opportunity to blacken the reputations of his defeated opponents, the Roman general Antony and the Egyptian queen Cleopatra. It was a process of propaganda which began before Actium, picked up pace after the deaths of Antony and Cleopatra, and has clouded every account of the period ever since. As is so often the case, truth was one of the first casualties of regime change.

To cloud matters even more, the story of Antony and Cleopatra's deaths quickly became the stuff of romantic legend, a 'real life' parallel to the myth of Pyramus and Thisbe (see pp. 164–5), a precursor to the tragedy of Romeo and Juliet – and so it has remained until the present day. In books, in paintings, on stage and in film, the doomed passion of these two powerful and flamboyant lovers has become iconic.

As the exotic glamour of the tale took over from hard history, and despite the evidence of coin portraits and descriptions by contemporary authors, so (predominantly male) historians' imaginings of Cleopatra's beauty ran riot, until they and their readers have become as captivated by her perceived allure as Augustus' propaganda once accused Antony of having been.

As a result, many books on Cleopatra written by career scribes and scholars, missed by life and love, for whom any whiff of sex or passion stirs up the self-reproach of childhoods spent in darkened dorms, read as if Cleopatra is a guilty pleasure, a secret avatar of an illicit mistress, as if (give them but half a chance) their authors would themselves like to lead her off to share their book-strewn beds. They fantasize about the colour of her eyes, the texture of her hair, the curve of her nose, the fullness of her lips, the shading of her skin, and no doubt more besides, which they cannot quite bring themselves to write about.

Shakespearean Lovers: Earthenware tile with Antony and Cleopatra, by John Moyr-Smith, c.1875. 15 x 15 cm. British Museum, 2000,1102.1, donated by Judith Ann Rudoe.

A further furtive thrill comes from the apparent immorality of key players in the story. It is perhaps true that Antony, exuberant, unscrupulous, in his own eyes the embodiment of Dionysus, would no doubt have embraced the philosophy of Alexis Zorbas in Kazantzakis' book that 'the greatest sin a man can commit is when a woman asks him to her bed, and he does not go'. Certainly it is true that Cleopatra bore children by men to whom she was not married. But although such behaviour might well have prompted past generations to exclaim 'how unlike, how very unlike, the home life of our own dear queen', such a scandalized reaction does little to help us understand the circumstances which led the most powerful politicians of their age to do the things they did. In fact, the prim and disapproving prism of later Christian ethics means that we must think very hard before we presume to judge the private life of any character from antiquity; when this is further skewed by the distorting lens of Augustan propaganda, it makes any moral judgements irrelevant.

Indeed, it is far from clear to what extent Antony and Cleopatra's relationship was based on love ('whatever', as a more recent royal has mused, 'love means'). Neither was so naïve as to believe that, in the words of one of Augustus' staff poets, 'love conquers everything', and each was experienced enough to know that, in politics, hard-headed decisions must always trump emotional responses, however attractive these may be.

For this reason, we have deliberately eschewed any reference to 'love' as a motivating force in Antony and Cleopatra's political partnership. This is not to say that we deny that there was any kind of emotional bond between the two; it is simply that we recognize that we do not (and cannot) know the true nature of that bond.

Instead, we have attempted to recount the events which led up to that fateful – if somewhat squalid – battle in the bay at Actium, to describe the personalities involved as well as the inexorable forces which drove them, and to suggest how the truth was massaged, if not completely misrepresented, by the victorious Augustus.

Throughout the book, we have tried to tell the story from the point of view of Alexandria, the extraordinary Greek city planted on the northern coast of Egypt, where for almost 300 years culture and hedonism had flourished side by side in a flowering of civilization which put Rome firmly in the shade (and which, as a result, most Romans both envied and meanly disparaged).

Like the rest of Egypt, Alexandria was dependent for food on the annual flooding of the Nile, a circumstance entirely outside her own control. How the city rode and reacted to the presence or absence of rainfall hundreds of miles to the south had determined her past success and made her rulers savvy to the vicissitudes of chance. And none more than Cleopatra. For her fate and that of Alexandria were intertwined, and it is in that remarkable city that our account begins.

CHAPTER 1

African Queen

ALEXANDRIA, EGYPT: MID-SEPTEMBER 31 BC

DAWN BREAKS, ALREADY WARM,[1] over the waking city.
As the sun rises higher in the molten sky, its rays bring into ever sharper
focus the buildings and the monuments laid out on their great grid across
the low-lying spit of land. Already, from the sea, the sun's light shines
more brightly than the dying flames of the Pharos, the gleaming marble
lighthouse towering to starboard, its mirrors high above the masts of ships
as they nudge their way inside the safety of the harbour.

From such a ship on such a morning, a first-time visitor
would have been wonder-struck. What first to look at? To the
ship's port-side, the royal palace, silhouetted sharply now
against the rising sun, the power-base of the Ptolemies,
with its own imperial harbour, a place of fabled wealth, of
marbled colonnades, cool fountained squares, of priceless
statuary and costly hangings, of vast prodigious luxury.
Signs of the Ptolemies are everywhere, not least here at the
harbour mouth, where two rose-granite statues, almost eight
times life-size, both of former queens, both with the name of
Cleopatra, watch over the approaching ships.

Then, from the palace, scanning round towards the south, the city
proper: the theatre on the hill; the Temple of Poseidon (Greek god of the
sea); the great Caesareum, the massive colonnaded complex built by the
present queen in honour of her world's most powerful man. The docks and
warehouses stretch far along the waterfront, already bustling with business
even at this early hour (though on this day, perhaps, men's tempers fray
more readily, for all know that their city's fate is hanging in the balance).
Far off in the haze stretches the long arched causeway of the Heptastadion,
which links the mainland to the Pharos island with its temple to the
universal goddess Isis and its lighthouse soaring more than 120 metres into
the dazzling sky; and beyond the Heptastadion another harbour, the distant
skyline bristling with masts, Eunostos, 'Harbour of a Safe Return'.

Opposite *Alexandria,
showing Canopic Street
looking west,* by J.P.
Golvin. Watercolour, after
Alexandria Rediscovered
(London 1998), p. 47.

Above A ship sails past
the Pharos. Copper-alloy
coin of Commodus (AD
180–192), struck at
Alexandria. Diam. 2.4 cm.
British Museum, G.2429.

The entrance to the ancient Great Harbour (now the East Harbour) at Alexandria from the site of the Pharos.

As his ship cut closer to the shore, the visitor might well have thought of all the other sights he might see. He would have known that Alexandria was famed for its wide airy boulevards, a grid of streets, its plan begun three centuries before, when the young Alexander, known now as 'the Great', had come here on campaign and resolved to build a new metropolis on the site of a pharaonic fishing town. Alexander had himself assigned the site, sufficiently close to the Nile delta that it might control trade from the Egyptian heartland, sufficiently removed that it would not be inundated by the river's annual floods. He had entrusted its design to his chief architect, Dinocrates, who in his turn assembled an outstanding team of specialist technicians, engineers and masters of hydraulics whose expertise ensured that water would flow as constantly throughout the low-lying city as the fresh breeze drifted through its summer streets.

It had been Alexander's vision that the city would become a great commercial centre at the hub of trade, an entrepôt to link the thriving markets of both the Greek mainland and the eastern coastal ports of

Ephesus, Miletus and Antioch with Egypt and the Nile, so that the economic potential of his embryonic empire might be exploited to the full. Within fifty years this had become reality. Alexandria grew so rapidly that, home to well over half a million people, it soon became the largest city in the ancient world.

After Alexander's early death, his fledgling empire had been divided between his generals. Egypt fell to Ptolemy, the founder of a colourful dynasty of kings and queens who ruled the vast land through a tightly controlled civil service, exploiting its wealth to the maximum, enriching its new capital. This first Ptolemy, called Soter (Saviour, c.367–c.283 BC), had intercepted Alexander's body as it was being conveyed back home to Macedonia from Babylon where he had died, and had brought it instead to Egypt. Now in the royal demesne at Alexandria, it lay in a glass case in a specially constructed mausoleum, the so-called Soma, the city's spiritual heart, a centre of pilgrimage, where its custody was deemed to justify the power held by its rulers. Over the years, the extent of that power had waxed and waned, but now, in 31 BC, thanks to the largesse of the Roman general Antony, the empire's boundaries stretched as far as they ever had: north to Cyprus, east to Syria and the coasts of modern Turkey, west to Cyrenaica, south down the Nile's umbilicus to Upper Egypt.

Three centuries after its foundation, the city, like the empire it controlled, teemed with a bewildering array of peoples: Greeks, of course, and native Egyptians, Jews and Syrians, Phoenicians and North Africans, its streets and wharves resounding to their polyglot hubbub. But from the start its citizens were strictly segregated in where they were allowed to go and where they might live. Alexandria was divided by class and ethnicity into five districts, each named, somewhat prosaically, after one of the first five letters of the Greek alphabet.

In District Alpha were the sprawling royal palaces, the gardens, the museum and the libraries. In Beta the Greek aristocracy could live, in Gamma the Greek commoners. Delta was for foreign settlers who were not Greek (from Persia or Syria, and Jews), while Epsilon was where the native population, the Egyptians, had their homes. It might have seemed a brilliant idea to Alexander and his architects. In fact, over the centuries, this ethnic segregation was to lead to tensions and to violence.

But Alexandria was to be known not simply for trade and economic wealth. Under the Ptolemies it would become the intellectual centre of the world. This intellectual life was focused on a building complex that

in its scale and ambition had no equal. The museum was quite literally a temple to the Muses, a centre for research and creativity, part university, part arts hub, part zoo and part botanic garden. At its core was the library, home to almost half a million volumes, papyrus scrolls arranged and catalogued with meticulous care, a copy (it was claimed) of every book of any significance which had ever been written.

So jealously did Alexandria's library guard its pre-eminence that the city kept a tight control over the export of papyrus reeds, a monopoly on the raw materials of book production. As a result, its greatest rival, the library at Pergamum in Anatolia, invented the new medium of parchment.

Alexandria's obsession with collecting books was legendary. Stories circulated of how special agents would examine cargoes of the ships docked in the harbour. If books were found they would be confiscated. According to one version, copies would be made and given to the owner, while the original was catalogued and filed in the library itself with the inscription 'from the ships'. Once, there had even been an international incident. Ptolemy III (Euergetes, r. 246–222 BC), eager to possess the dramatic works of Aeschylus, Sophocles and Euripides, had sent to Athens (where they were then stored), asking to borrow them for the purpose of making sumptuous copies. He offered fifteen talents of silver, a fabulous amount of money, as surety. But instead of sending back the originals as promised, he returned the copies, happily allowing the Athenians to keep the silver. To him, the manuscripts he now possessed at Alexandria were priceless.[2]

It was not only Greek literature that was collected here. In an unprecedented project, Ptolemy II (Philadelphus, r. 283–246 BC) arranged for seventy-two Jewish elders to produce their own Greek versions of the Torah, which were then collated into a definitive text, known as the Septuagint. How interested in all of this the Chief Librarian was, we do not know. At the time, this coveted position was held by the accomplished poet Apollonius, originally from Rhodes and now remembered for his epic about Jason and the Argonauts. In fact, the Chief Librarian did not need to be a literary man at all. Apollonius' successor was a scientist, Eratosthenes (c.276–195 BC), who calculated the circumference of the earth with remarkable accuracy.

Ptolemy I Soter. Fragment of a basalt Egyptian-style statue, Graeco-Roman, 305–283 BC. Height 64 cm. British Museum, 1914,0216.1.

Alexandria was a hotbed of new discoveries. Working at the museum, one of Eratosthenes' close contemporaries, the astronomer Aristarchus (*c*.310–230 BC), had already proposed a radical new theory: that the spherical earth rotates round the sun. Meanwhile, in the museum's medical school, surgeons such as Herophilus (335–280 BC) and Erasistratus (304–250 BC) were revolutionizing the understanding of blood flow and the brain through the dissection of human corpses and, more controversially, through the vivisection of condemned prisoners. If the screams of these unfortunates were offensive to the ears, in another laboratory more mellifluous sounds could be heard as the inventor Ctesibius (*fl.* 285–222 BC) performed on his new creation, the *hydraulis* or water organ, the world's first keyboard instrument. He also perfected the water clock, painstakingly defining the accuracy of timekeeping, even as, on a more cosmic scale, Eratosthenes was reforming the calendar, rationalizing the many ancient but messy lunar and solar computations and introducing the concept of the leap year.

But the museum was not Alexandria. Within its walls might be the greatest collection of books and intellectuals in the Greek-speaking world. Within its gardens might be examples of as many animals and plants as could be kept alive and studied by its scholars. But outside on the streets the atmosphere was altogether different.

For, despite its intellectual core, Alexandria in 31 BC was a city given over to the flesh and the imagination, a place of pleasure and of spectacle. The Ptolemies, who had ruled here for the past 300 years, thrived on theatricality and ostentatious display. People still remembered the midwinter procession of Ptolemy II (Philadelphus), the king who had commissioned the translation of the Torah. Held in Alexandria's hippodrome, the spectacle had been conceived in honour of Dionysus, the god not only of wine and drama but of fertility and life, the god moreover whose worship had taken hold throughout the Eastern Mediterranean, not least because of the promise he appeared to offer his worshippers of resurrection after death. In the centuries which followed, descriptions of the procession's opulence grew more florid with each retelling, until no one really knew what had been real and what mere make-believe:

> Silenoi [rampantly male creatures with the ears and legs of a horse or goat], costumed in riding cloaks, some of purple, others of red, led the procession. Their job was to control the crowds. Close behind came Satyrs [younger Silenoi]. There were 20 at each end of the stadium, and all carried torches decorated with gilt ivy leaves. Next came golden-winged Victories, bearing censers, three metres tall and also decorated with gilt ivy leaves, girls in short embroidered

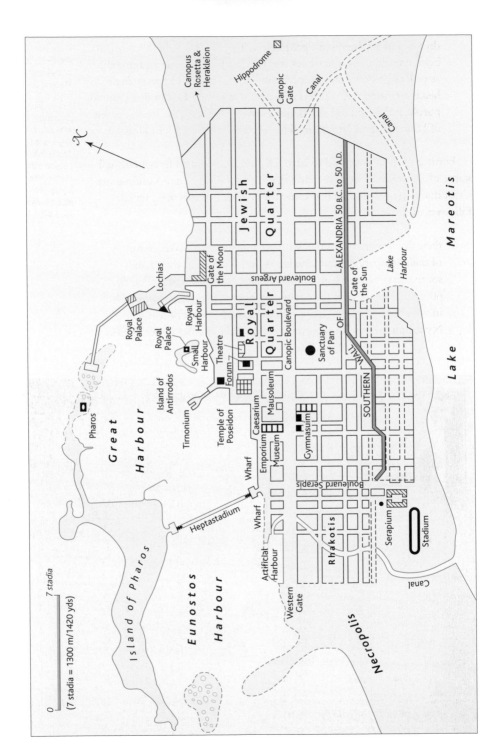

Canopus
Rosetta &
Herakleion

Hippodrome

Canopic
Gate

Canal

Canal

Jewish Quarter

ALEXANDRIA 50 B.C. to 50 A.D.

Boulevard Argeus

Gate of
the Moon

Lochias

Royal
Palace

Royal
Harbour

Royal
Palace

Small
Harbour

Island of
Antirrodos

Royal Quarter

Theatre

Forum

Canopic Boulevard

Gate of
the Sun

Lake
Harbour

Pharos

Great Harbour

Timonium

Temple of
Poseidon

Caesarium

Mausoleum

Museum

Emporium

Gymnasium

Sanctuary of Pan

SOUTHERN WALL OF

Lake

Wharf

Heptastadium

Wharf

Artificial
Harbour

Western
Gate

Rhakotis

Boulevard Serapis

Serapium

Stadium

Canal

Lake Mareotis

Island of Pharos

Eunostos Harbour

Necropolis

7 stadia

0

(7 stadia = 1300 m/1420 yds)

N

dresses and adorned with golden jewellery ... After them came 120 boys, dressed in purple tunics and bearing frankincense and myrrh, as well as golden plates heaped with saffron. Next, 40 Satyrs, their heads crowned with circlets of golden ivy leaves, their bodies painted purple and bright red ... Behind walked Philiscus, the poet, a priest of Dionysus, and with him all the guild of the Actors of Dionysus.

Further marvels were said to have followed, including a five-metre-tall statue of Dionysus himself, draped in gold and pouring wine, standing on a cart drawn by 180 men. Then came the Maenads, the ecstatic female followers of the god,

their flowing hair crowned with circlets, some of snakes, some of trailing asparagus and vine leaves and ivy. And in their hands some carried daggers, and others snakes. Behind them, pulled by 60 men, there came a four-wheeled wagon, four metres in width, in which was a seated statue of [the personification of Mount] Nysa, four metres tall, wearing a saffron robe adorned with golden

Opposite Plan of Alexandria in the first centuries BC/AD (After Macleod 2000, p. viii).

Below Dionysiac procession: a maenad with a drum and two satyrs, one playing a double-flute, the other carrying a thyrsus. Marble relief from near Rome, c. AD 100. Height 58.5 cm. British Museum, 1805,0703.128.

stars and draped in a Spartan shawl. The statue was able to rise up automatically without anyone touching it and, after pouring a libation of milk from a shallow golden dish, to sit down again. Next came another wagon, again four-wheeled, but this time ten metres long, eight wide, and pulled by 300 men. On it was a wine-press, twelve metres long and seven and a half wide, piled high with grapes, which 60 Satyrs (supervised by a Silenus) were treading as they sang a vintage hymn accompanied by flutes. A trail of new wine followed them the length of the procession. Then came a four-wheeled wagon, twelve and a half metres long, eight metres wide and pulled by 600 men. It carried a wine-skin sewn from leopard skins and with a capacity of 30,000 gallons, and it, too, trickled wine along the entire length of the procession.

From other statues on other carts milk and wine flowed out, as the procession made its seemingly never-ending progress into the stadium. In making the floating statue of Nysa, the boffins from the museum had clearly been busy, but they were not the only members of that institution who were involved. Elephants, drawn no doubt from the museum zoo, pulled chariots; so too did a whole menagerie of other creatures from camels to ostriches and from antelopes to billy-goats. The extravagance of the spectacle was breathtaking: camels carrying plates heaped high with spices; black African princes bearing tribute made up of 600 ivory tusks, 2,000 logs of ebony, bowls filled with coins and gold dust; 150 men, each carrying a tree containing caged animals and birds; and further droves of exotic beasts, snow white oxen from India, fourteen leopards, a rhinoceros, a giraffe, a large white she-bear.

> One wagon transported a 45-metre-long golden thyrsus [a stave sacred to Dionysus, wrapped with wool and ivy and thought to have magical properties]; another a 30-metre-long silver spear; yet another a 90-metre-long gold phallus, painted in a variety of colours, wrapped in gold bands and with a gold star, three metres across, at its tip.[3]

This was religion and showmanship on a quite breathtaking scale, a demonstration to the peoples of Alexandria and Egypt, not to mention of the Mediterranean world and beyond, of the wealth and ingenuity of the Ptolemies. Or so the Ptolemies would have it known.

For theirs was a dynasty which liked to do things on an heroic scale. One of Philadelphus' successors, Ptolemy IV (Philopator, r. 221–205 BC), used some of his almost limitless resources to build (some said) the largest boat in antiquity. Its entire hull decorated with encaustic paintings of

Dionysiac motifs, the ship was 140 metres long, had 40 banks of oars, and the top of its stern-post rose 26 metres above sea level.

> Its trial voyage needed 4,000 oarsmen (with 400 in reserve). 2,850 marines were on deck and there were more below, along with a vast amount of equipment. It was launched from a kind of cradle, constructed (so they say) from the timbers of 50 large warships and dragged into the water by a multitude of men, urged on by shouting and the blare of trumpets.

But even more famous was Philopator's river boat, the so-called cabin-carrier, in which he cruised the River Nile. One hundred metres long, the yacht was nothing less than a floating palace, with saloons for fine dining, bedrooms, promenades and shrines to the gods, all made from cypress and cedar wood imported from the Levant, and ornamented in ivory, copper and gold.

> The banqueting room had a beautiful coffered ceiling made out of gilded cypress wood and with sculpted ornamentation. Next to this was sleeping accommodation with seven berths. An adjacent companionway led up to . . . a rotunda-shaped shrine to Aphrodite, which contained a marble statue of the goddess. Opposite this was another opulent banqueting room lined with columns in Indian marble. Towards the prow was an apartment sacred to Dionysus, also columned, and with space for thirteen couches. Its cornice was gilded as far as the architrave, and the ceiling was decorated as befits the god . . . The mast was 35 metres high with a fine linen sail augmented by a purple topsail.[4]

Just as the museum was not Alexandria, so Alexandria was not Egypt, as cruises down the Nile would have reminded the Ptolemies and their guests. As they sailed further from the Mediterranean, away from the Delta and into the country's heartland, they must have felt as if they were entering an alien world. True, Greeks had been frequent visitors for centuries. Readers of Homer (as all Greeks were) had long been familiar with tales of how the mythical king Menelaus had come here, blown off course on his voyage home from Troy. And the story had soon sprung up that Helen, his beguiling wife whose fateful beauty had enflamed the Trojan Paris and so begun a lengthy war, had spent the entire duration of the campaign in Egypt – the gods had packed a phantom Helen off to Troy, letting the real woman live in luxury for ten years by the seductive banks of the Nile.

In historic times, Greek merchants had established an early trading post on the Delta at Naucratis, where they exchanged timber, silver, olive oil and wine for Egyptian goods such as linen and papyrus. However, it was the 'peculiar beauty' of the city's prostitutes that struck the Greek historian Herodotus when he visited the city in the fifth century BC.[5] Yet even they were not enough to detain him. Showing an enthusiasm which would infect Greek and Roman visitors for generations, he travelled as far south as Elephantine (for map, see p. 36), seeing the sights, questioning the priests, taking notes of all he had been told, both true and demonstrably false. He devoted an entire book (one of the nine in his *Histories*) to Egypt, discussing matters as varied as crocodiles and phoenixes, pygmies and pyramids (already over two millennia old by the time he saw them, and faced in dazzling white limestone). The country fascinated him. He immersed himself in the arcane practices of mummification; had the priests read to him from their ancient records, which already listed names of no fewer than 330 pharaohs. He listened awestruck to a story of an army sent out on campaign that marched into the desert and was never seen again.

Epitomizing the wonder of Egypt was the behaviour of the River Nile. Its annual inundation struck Herodotus (as it did everyone) as nothing short of miraculous, a gift of fecundity in an otherwise barren land which must come from the gods. His eyewitness account reminds us of the sheer wonderment of the phenomenon:

> When the Nile floods, only the cities remain above water, looking very like Aegean islands, standing isolated, while the rest of the land becomes a sea. When this happens, people are ferried in boats not only along the river but across the plains. Indeed, a voyage from Naucratis to Memphis passes right by the pyramids themselves . . .

To Herodotus, Egypt was nothing less than the 'gift of the Nile', whose alluvial mud rendered the land the most fertile and productive of any he had visited. Indeed, the great expanses of golden cornfields which lined the riverbank were both a blessing and a threat to Egypt. In the years before Alexander, the Persians had occupied the land, drawn by the potential of its soil, and now, in the years around 31 BC, it was again an object of desire. With hungry mouths to feed, the politicians of Rome had been increasingly turning their voracious eyes towards the harvests of the Nile and calculating how best to appropriate them for their own citizens' consumption. The past century had seen an uneasy relationship develop between the two great empires, as it became increasingly clear that the relatively peaceable Egypt needed to treat her warlike rival with great care, forcing generations of Ptolemaic kings and queens to walk a dangerous diplomatic tightrope as they decided which Roman statesman they should court, which they should shun.

To foreigners such as the Romans, or the Greek historian Herodotus, nothing about Egypt and the Egyptians seemed familiar; indeed, everything appeared to be the opposite of what they were used to.

In their country, it is the women who engage in buying and selling, while the men stay at home and weave ...Women urinate standing up, men sitting down. They relieve themselves indoors, but eat outside on the streets, arguing that anything which is shameful but essential should be hidden, but anything not shameful should be done openly ... Elsewhere priests have long hair; in Egypt they are shaved.

'Gift of the Nile': cattle are driven towards a scribe who records them in a ledger. Wall-painting from the Tomb of Nebamun, Thebes, c.1350 BC. Height 58.5 cm; width 97 cm. British Museum, EA 37976.

They had a bewildering attitude to animals, too.

Each type of animal has its own guardian appointed to feed them, in the case of one a man, in that of another a woman ... If anyone deliberately kills such an animal, the penalty is death ... All members of a household where a cat has died a natural death, shave their eyebrows; but when a dog dies they shave their entire bodies. In the city of Bubastis, dead cats are carried into sacred buildings, where they are embalmed and buried.

23

All this, he realized, was part of their religion, and Herodotus' reaction when faced with so many alien and animal-headed gods was (typically for a Greek) to try to equate them with the gods he knew and worshipped himself. Certain rituals and rites seemed very familiar to him, like one he compared with Greek processions in honour of Dionysus,

> except for the dances. Instead of the phallus they have devised puppets which are moved by strings, about 45 centimetres tall, which the women carry round the villages. These puppets have fully-moving male members, almost as big as the rest of their bodies. A flute player leads the procession and all the women follow on, singing hymns to Dionysus. There is a sacred legend which provides a reason for the size and motions of the puppets' genitals.

The similarity (albeit on a smaller scale) with Ptolemy II's great procession in the hippodrome at Alexandria is striking – even down to the moving statues – and this practice of assimilating the Egyptian and Greek religions was something the Ptolemies encouraged with great energy. For political reasons, they considered it important that the peoples whom they governed, Greeks and Egyptians, adhered to roughly the same belief system – especially since the native Egyptians had fewer rights and were subject to greater legal strictures than their new colonial overlords. The increasing trend away from the worship of a multiplicity of minor deities towards a belief in a few all-powerful gods (typified in the Greek East by Dionysus) made this process all the easier. Ptolemy I even went so far as to invent an entirely new god, Serapis, Greek in appearance but with many Egyptian properties, around which he hoped his new subjects would unite. Despite lavish temples to the new god in Alexandria itself, his worship never entirely caught on, and subsequent Ptolemies were more concerned with highlighting parallels between existing gods, equating the Egyptian deity Isis with the Greek goddesses Hera, Aphrodite and Demeter, and her consort, Osiris, whose death and resurrection were celebrated annually, with Dionysus.

Isis and Osiris became the two chief deities of Ptolemaic Egypt, and their popularity spread across the Mediterranean. The myths which surrounded them and their son Horus promised life everlasting. Osiris, the mortal husband of Isis, goddess of fertility and magic, was murdered, his body divided into fourteen parts and scattered across Egypt. Isis, distraught, searched for each of them but found only thirteen. The phallus remained lost. Still, Isis succeeded in reforming Osiris from the collected parts and breathed life back into him. Despite her husband's loss, Isis still managed to produce a son, Horus, and the image of mother and child became universally enduring. In time, the resurrected Osiris became king of the dead, Horus of the living, while the fecund mother goddess Isis, protector of her people, became known in the Egyptian *Book of the Dead* as 'she who gives birth to heaven and earth, who knows the orphan, who knows the widow; she who seeks justice for the poor, shelter for the weak and righteousness in her people'.

In trying to unite the Greek and Egyptian religions, the Ptolemies went further than any had before them. For a long time, it had been usual in the east, though not in Greece, for rulers to be worshipped as if they themselves were gods. It was a practice that the flamboyant Alexander the Great and his successors embraced enthusiastically. Thus the Ptolemies slipped effortlessly into the role enjoyed by past dynasties of pharaohs before them and allowed themselves to be venerated as the divine embodiment of the fertility of Egypt and the aspirations of its people. And this in turn led to their engaging in another practice wholly alien to Greek tradition: marriage between siblings.

The Egyptian deities Isis and Osiris, as well as being husband and wife, were also brother and sister. Now, as the living personification of those deities, the Ptolemies mirrored their marital arrangements too, with the result that for some seven generations, with only a few exceptions, its members married and mated exclusively within their own immediate family. Not that this necessarily made them well disposed to one another. Throughout its history, the Ptolemaic dynasty was characterized by the imaginative ways in which family members contrived to have each other killed. Yet, thanks to a combination of luck, guile and a ruthlessly efficient (if at times corrupt) civil service, the Ptolemies survived, wielding their autocratic power not only in the Egyptian hinterland, where they were rarely seen, but in their gilded capital at Alexandria and in the satellite cities which dotted the coast of the Nile delta.

These cities, too, played their part (not least through acts of calculated theatricality) in bolstering the mystic aura of the ruling dynasty and its connection to the ancient rituals of Egypt. At Herakleion, a port on the coast a few miles north-east of Alexandria, also on a spit of land between a lake and the sea, was the temple of the Greek god Herakles in which the Ptolemies (who claimed descent from him) were crowned. Yet in the statues they erected there, some as many as five metres tall, they chose to show themselves in classic Egyptian style: the kings bare-chested, wearing only the traditional loincloth, their arms held stiffly by their sides, left leg advanced, their heads crowned by the *pschent*, the double diadem which symbolized the unity of Upper and Lower Egypt, a cobra coiled above their brows; the queens dressed in transparent clinging robes, on their bewigged heads the Hathoric crown, complete with cow horns, feathers and a sun disc.

From Herakleion every year, once the seeds had begun to sprout, a sacred ship sailed west on a canal cut to Canopus, a symbolic voyage which reflected not just the journey of the sun and moon across the sky but the path of life from its beginning to its end. Walking on the shore, worshippers accompanied the ship, on which were placed two effigies of the god Osiris, one made from vegetables and grains, the other from minerals, tokens of the great fecundity not only of the god but of the land of Egypt itself.

As the geographer Strabo observed, Canopus, the destination of the pilgrimage, was not simply a religious centre.

> Here is the greatly revered temple of Serapis. Such are the cures effected here that even the most respectable men have faith in it and come to sleep here. As if to make up for this, crowds of revellers sail by canal to Canopus from Alexandria for public festivals. Day and night alike it is crowded with people on boats, playing the flute and dancing wildly and with the utmost depravity – men and women alike, and the inhabitants of Canopus, too, who have special areas near the canal specifically equipped for this kind of entertainment and debauchery.[6]

From Canopus, another canal led back to the suburbs of Alexandria itself and to the hippodrome, once the site of Ptolemy II's Dionysiac parade. From here a monumental archway, the Canopic Gate, opened onto one of the widest boulevards of any city in the ancient world. Thirty metres wide, it marked a pinnacle of sophistication. Flanked as it was on either side by the cool shade of glittering limestone colonnades, it ran the width of Alexandria as far as the western suburb of Necropolis, with its groves and gardens and its chapels dedicated to the esoteric art of mummification. At regular intervals the boulevard, its buildings in coloured stone, pink, green and black, was intersected by side streets, themselves some seven metres wide, those to the north leading towards the city's harbours, those to the south towards the great lagoon of Lake Mareotis.

If the harbours gave Alexandria her link to the outside world, Lake Mareotis formed part of the umbilical cord that connected her (by canals dug to the Delta) to the very core of Egypt. It was to this lake that boats laden with grain and other produce would ply their way down the Nile, their cargoes to be offloaded, checked and stored in the massive granaries and warehouses which lined its banks. Here too, on the muddy shores of the lemon-mauve lake, the haunt of countless water birds, was the industrial quarter of the city, the home of glassmakers and potters, weavers and wine traders.

With its law courts and its temples, its gymnasia and palaces, the architects of Alexandria had created a city of infinite complexity and inexhaustible fascination. To allow it to be viewed in its entirety, they had even built an artificial hill, the so-called Paneium, constructed in the shape of a fir-cone, ascended by a spiral road, from whose summit could be had a panoramic view of the whole of the city. From here Alexandria, bounded as it was on one side by the shimmering sea, and on the other by the desert, both inhospitable and stretching through the heat haze to their own horizon, must have seemed like a mirage or an oasis, a flowering of civilization on the fringes of a wilderness.

However, on that September day in 31 BC, the chances are that the summit of the Paneium was empty, the city streets, too, preternaturally quiet, the shops of the Canopic Boulevard closed, their windows shuttered, their owners like the rest of the multitudes of Alexandria lined up along the harbour wall. For the news had come that all had been expecting for so long. The months of uncertainty were over. Watched anxiously by so many countless thousands, the first of the fleet of proud rich-painted warships, its bows hung with garlands of fresh flowers, even now was entering the royal harbour, its oars like great wings beating rhythmically as it approached the quay. As the ships came closer, it may be that on a given order all the oars in unison rose in salute, held for a long moment high in the air, dripping their wake of molten silver into the shimmering sunlight of the harbour. This was the signal that the onlookers were waiting for, the sign of triumph, the token clear to all that Cleopatra, Queen Of Kings, Whose Sons Are Kings, The Younger Goddess, Father-Loving, Lover Of Her Fatherland, latest of the line of Ptolemies, had come back to her city, Alexandria, to proclaim that far away at Actium in Greece she and her consort, the Roman general Mark Antony, had fought against Octavian. And won.

CHAPTER 2

Marked Woman

ALEXANDRIA: EARLY AUTUMN 48 BC

THE BEAT OF OARS had marked the rhythm of Cleopatra's life, and as the queen in her garland-festooned galley glided into the royal harbour on that September day of 31 BC, she may perhaps have thought back to another entrance (and one equally calculated to impress) that she had made some seventeen years earlier. Then, as the sun perhaps was setting and the oil lamps were being lit across the city, a tiny fishing boat had rowed in through the harbour mouth. To any onlooker it had been but one among many. A single boatman worked the oars, steering towards the royal harbour, where Roman warships rode at anchor, guiding his craft between their tarry hulls.

At the wharf-side, when he tied up, he had carefully lifted out what seemed to be a long slim canvas bag and hoisted it with care across his shoulders. No doubt answering demands for passwords to the satisfaction of the guards, he had been escorted through the palace gates, along the corridors and into the imperial reception room and the presence of the Roman general. Then, bending down, the boatman had drawn his knife and cut the cords with which the bag was tied, folding back the canvas to reveal its delightfully bewitching (if somewhat ruffled) contents. The ruse had worked. The blockade had been breached. Cleopatra, the deposed queen of Egypt, had come to plead her case before great Caesar.

The Ptolemaic dynasty, to which Cleopatra belonged, had already enjoyed a long if occasionally stormy relationship with Rome. In Egypt itself, the dynasty's grip on the throne had always threatened to be tenuous. Even in the Delta, rebellions had broken out, and not only among the indigenous population. After one particularly brutal episode, the priests at Memphis had published a decree outlining punishments imposed on unsuccessful rebels (196 BC). Written in Greek, Egyptian Demotic and hieroglyphs, its words were clearly aimed at a wide multi-cultural audience.[7] A generation or so later (164 BC), two rival Ptolemies had tried (both unsuccessfully) to win Rome's backing for their cause, but it was

Evidence of rebellion: the Rosetta Stone records a decree of Ptolemy V issued in 196 BC, written in hieroglyphic, Demotic and Greek texts. Granodiorite, from Egypt. Height 112.3 cm; width 75.7 cm. British Museum, EA 24, donated by King George III.

during the reign of the next king, Ptolemy VIII (182–116 BC), that Egypt really came within Rome's orbit.

This Ptolemy was a grotesque. Nicknamed 'the Dumpling' by the Alexandrians, he was hideously fat, sexually insatiable and so averse to the intellectuals who opposed him that he had caused the museum to be virtually shut down. Yet he opened up Alexandria to Rome, going so far as to meet one delegation at the harbour, dressed in his trademark see-through robes. The Romans, fascinated by his flab, forced him to waddle with them through the city streets, joking (behind his sizeable back) that the Alexandrians were now in their debt for providing such a spectacle. But it was with the fat of the land that the delegates were most impressed. Egypt once visited, the Romans would return.

In time Alexandria became used to hosting political and trade missions from far-off Italy, entertaining their members lavishly with cruises up the Nile to view the pyramids or feed the sacred crocodiles. Rome, after all, was a lucrative market and the more favourable the terms and the more easy the conditions with which the Egyptians did business, the less inevitable the Ptolemies hoped it might be that the aggressively expanding empire would wish to annex their land. In fact, Rome's senate viewed with trepidation the idea of occupying Egypt – the land was simply too rich: whoever was sent to govern it might grow too powerful.

Already by the late second century BC Rome's power was formidable. In 146 BC, her armies had won victories against two great trading rivals: Corinth in the Greek east and Carthage which had controlled the seas to the south and west. Almost overnight, Rome had become the dominant player in the Mediterranean. Countries bordering her empire looked on with fear. To avoid what he predicted would be a bloody invasion after his death, one ruler went so far as to bequeath his entire kingdom to Rome: Pergamum, the city whose bookish interests had brought it into direct competition with Alexandria (133 BC). Yet, her unprecedented power was not to cause Rome's new subjects, or even her own citizens, unfettered joy.

The next years saw first the lower classes (plebeians) of Rome herself and then her allies within Italy begin to fight for a share in her new-found power and riches (91–87 BC). If this were not enough, Rome's most dominant generals and politicians embarked on a series of devastating civil wars to try to win the greatest prize of all: total power over the emergent empire. In a conflict which was to form the blueprint for three generations, two men, Marius and Sulla, both veterans of the war with the Italian allies, pitted their legions against each other in a bid to gain control of Rome (88–87 BC). At last, Marius' death (86 BC) left Sulla in the supreme position for which he had struggled for so long, and for which, too, he had ordered the execution of so many of his rivals, their names inscribed on grim proscription lists. Then, surprisingly, only five years later, Sulla retired to write his memoirs. Three years later, he too was dead.

In the aftermath of this first civil war, an uneasy peace blanketed the empire. Gradually, though, two further rivals rose through the ranks, each in his own way connected to one of the former generals. Gnaeus Pompey had been a lieutenant in Sulla's army; Julius Caesar was related through marriage to Marius. For a time, their chosen paths to power kept them apart as Pompey roved the trouble-spots of empire with his troops, single-handedly (or so he would have it believed) defeating the enemies of Rome wherever he might find them.

Caesar, meanwhile, was playing a more political game, rising through the ranks, making alliances, doing deals. Of course, he had his detractors,

men who poured scorn on his louche dress-sense (he liked to wear his tunic fringed and long and loosely tied) or his exotic love life (he was said to have given pleasure to the king of Bithynia). None of this had held him back, and by 59 BC Caesar and Pompey, sensing danger if they did not do so, entered into an unofficial pact to further each other's interests. Moderating the two men was a third, the fabulously wealthy banker, Publius Crassus. The deal was sealed; Caesar gave Pompey his daughter Julia's hand in marriage, and himself embarked on a series of dangerous but high-profile military campaigns in Germany and Gaul.

Ptolemy XII 'the Flautist': silver *tetradrachm* minted in Egypt, 80–51 BC. Diam. 2.6 cm. British Museum, 1987,0649.520.

Yet, even gripped by monumental rivalries, Rome was a force to be reckoned with, and the Ptolemies seemed determined to embroil that empire's politicians in their own domestic affairs. In 58 BC another Ptolemy (XII) turned up in the eternal city, the self-styled 'New Dionysus'. The Alexandrians (some of whom nicknamed him 'the Flautist', others less imaginatively 'the Bastard') had objected strongly to what they saw as his weakness in allowing Rome to appropriate from his brother the island of Cyprus – especially since he had earlier paid massive bribes to secure the support of Rome's richest and most powerful men, Crassus, Caesar and Pompey.

Thus, with Alexandria in turmoil, it was to the house of his creditor Pompey in Rome that the Flautist fled. Feelings among the senatorial elite were mixed, but those who had made lucrative loans to Ptolemy calculated that, unless he was restored to the Egyptian throne, he would be unable to repay them. Loath to involve Rome in direct military intervention (they cited an oracle which suggested that such action would end in disaster), Ptolemy's creditors generously allowed him to take out further loans to pay 2,000 mercenaries. Under the command of Aulus Gabinius, a staunch supporter of Pompey, these hired men defeated the Egyptian insurgents and restored the Flautist to his throne (55 BC). Back in the royal palace at Alexandria, Ptolemy executed his eldest daughter, who had shown herself too ready to step into his shoes, and, retaining his mercenaries, the so-called Gabinians, resumed his life of luxury, of

> general licentiousness, practising the accompaniment of dances on his flute and . . . holding dance contests in his palace.[8]

It was now that, to help take care of the actual running of his kingdom, he appointed as co-ruler his eldest surviving daughter, a girl possessed of exceptional talent and a remarkable capacity to adapt and to survive, a fourteen year-old who was possibly already more experienced in politics than many adults, and in whose reign Rome would become an ever more important player on the stage of Alexandria and Egypt: Cleopatra.

In the years to come, Cleopatra would prove herself to be the very embodiment of Alexandria: elegant, cool, educated, international, but with the potential, when the situation demanded, to let her hair down and carouse. A woman of extraordinary intellect, she was not only a brilliant linguist, the first of all her dynasty to learn to speak Egyptian, but a polymath who regularly attended the debates in the museum, who understood the secrets of politics and power more dazzlingly than any of her rivals. For she knew she had one crucial asset, which set her uniquely apart: her seductive magnetism.

Perhaps she was not the most outstanding beauty of her age (though there are sources which suggest she was most beautiful), but her bewitching eyes and her alluring voice, her wit, her charm, her conversation and her humour,[9] would all be used to maximum effect to try to win round her kingdom and to keep it for herself. Which was just as well. For, almost from the first, she found herself in difficulties.

In March 51 BC, Ptolemy XII, the New Dionysus, Father-loving God, Brother-loving God, also called the Flautist, died. Egyptian tradition dictated that Cleopatra could not rule alone, so, in accordance with their father's wishes, within weeks the eighteen-year-old queen found herself not only sharing the throne with her ten-year-old brother Ptolemy XIII (the Father-loving God) but married to him. It was not a situation which appealed to her. By August the same year, she was already trying to sideline her brother and assert her independence by issuing coinage and decrees in her own name. It was an unwise move. Alexandria was a hotbed of factions, of eunuchs and advisers, soldiers and civil servants all jockeying for power, and, in the months and years which followed the Flautist's death, an increasing number of them began to side with the boy Ptolemy XIII. No doubt they thought he would be so much easier to manipulate than his spirited, ambitious sister.

Already by 50 BC, Cleopatra had lost the loyalty of the Gabinian mercenaries, brought by her father from Rome some five years earlier. When these Gabinians murdered the sons of a Roman consul, who had come to Alexandria requesting their help in an eastern war, Cleopatra found herself faced by a difficult choice: to upset the troops on whose support she relied for domestic law and order, or to risk the wrath of

Julius Caesar: iron finger-ring with a gilded emblem, perhaps the property of one of his followers in the civil war following his assassination. Roman, c.42 BC. Diam. 2.6 cm. British Museum, 1873,1020.4.

Rome. The latter was more dangerous. She arrested those responsible for the murder and had them extradited.

Yet, this was only the beginning of Cleopatra's troubles. Her father, the Flautist, had been profligate with money; he had left behind a legacy of debt; and now, at a time of economic melt-down, the Nile floods failed and with them, crucially, the harvests. Unrest stalked the streets of Alexandria. Led by the unctious eunuch Pothinus, the faction which controlled young Ptolemy XIII staged a *coup d'état* (sometime around 48 BC). Cleopatra, together with Arsinoë, her younger sister, fled from the city east towards the frontier town Pelusium, where she raised whatever troops she could and prepared to make a stand. In truth, though, she must have thought the game was over.

And so it would have been, had not Rome and the affairs of her empire intervened in a most unexpected way. For a time the pact between Pompey and Caesar had endured. Then, while Caesar was on campaign in far off Britain, his daughter Julia (whom he had married to his rival, Pompey) died (54 BC); the next year, the pact's mediator Crassus, believing perhaps that he could emulate his colleagues' prowess on the battle field, launched a quite unprovoked attack east against the mighty Parthian Empire. He should have stuck to banking. His army was defeated, its talismanic eagle standards lost, and the Parthian king celebrated (appropriately enough) by pouring molten gold down the dead Crassus' throat. The dead banker's severed head was said to have been later (though, one hopes, not *much* later) used as a prop in a production of Euripides' *Bacchae*. Events moved swiftly. Within four years (49 BC), Caesar had led his campaign-hardened legions across the Rubicon and into Italy, while Pompey and a flock of timorous senators fled to Greece to rally troops. After a series of hard-fought battles, the two sides met at Pharsalus, the capital of which, Homeric Phthia, had been home to Alexander the Great's role-model, the hero Achilles. In a fittingly epic encounter, Caesar's troops prevailed (48 BC). Pompey himself fled, first to the island of Lesbos and then, with his wife and family safe on board and with Caesar only a few days behind him, on a swift ship heading south.

His goal was Egypt and the court of Ptolemy XIII. After all, Pompey reckoned, when Ptolemy's father, the Flautist, had been forced into exile from Alexandria, had he not offered sanctuary

A young Cleopatra already seems burdened by responsibility: silver *tetradrachm*, struck at Ascalon in Palestine, in 50/49 BC. Diam. 2.6 cm. British Museum, 1875,1102.3.

in his own house? Had he not argued the Egyptian's cause? Had he not lent him money? Indeed, had not Ptolemy XIII himself sent a fleet of fifty warships to help Pompey only months before? The ties between the families were strong, and Egypt was a wealthy country whose resources Pompey could use to great advantage in the next phase of his war with Caesar.

By the time Pompey's warship reached the coast of Egypt, Ptolemy XIII had already set out with his army for Pelusium, just days away from the battle in which he hoped to deliver the final *coup de grâce* to his sister Cleopatra. Now, by the shore near Mount Casius, some thirty miles east of the Nile delta, the young king had pitched camp; while out to sea, his ship riding lazily at anchor on the limpid waters, Pompey prepared to disembark.

It was in these crucial moments that Ptolemy and his advisers made a gross miscalculation, the consequences of which, unimaginable at the time, would have a more profound impact upon their kingdom than any taken in the 300 years before. In a hastily convened conference, they debated what to do with Pompey. News of Pharsalus had reached them, and with it reports that the victorious Caesar was already on his way. The last thing anybody wanted was Rome's civil war being played out on Egyptian soil. In the meeting's closing moments, the ghastly Pothinus made a grim pronouncement: 'Dead men don't bite'. The final sentence had been passed on Pompey.

Even on board the warship, as he saw the small boat which was to take him ashore being rowed out to meet him, Pompey sensed danger. Despite the smiles of the six men on board, one of whom, Septimius, he recognized, something seemed wrong. On shore, armed men stood ready; at sea, the Ptolemaic warships seemed to be closing in. Pompey knew it was a trap, yet there was nothing he could do. He embraced his wife and stepped into the boat, his last words a quotation from the Greek dramatist Sophocles:

> Even if he was a free man beforehand,
> Whoever enters a tyrant's court becomes a slave.

The biographer Plutarch described what happened next:

> It was some distance from the warship to the shore. As not one of those on board spoke a single friendly word to him, Pompey looked at Septimius and said: 'Unless I'm much mistaken, we served together, you and I.' Septimius nodded grimly but said nothing. Silence. Pompey took out a little scroll, in which he had written a speech in Greek which he meant to use when addressing Ptolemy, and began to leaf through it. As they came near the shore, his wife, Cornelia,

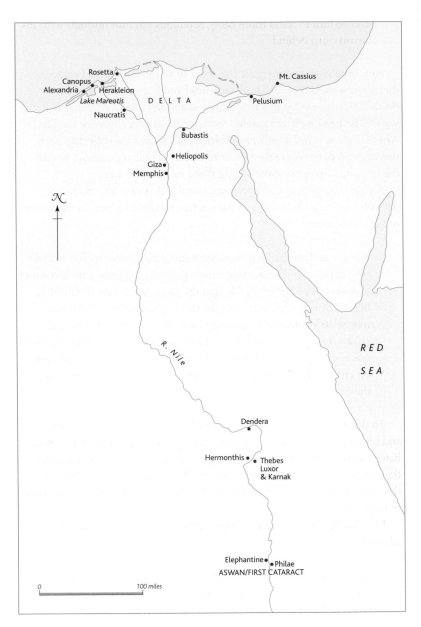

Map of Egypt showing
the sites mentioned in
the text.

and his friends watched from the warship to see what would happen.
Cornelia was very anxious, but she began to take heart when she
saw great numbers of Ptolemy's attendants gathering together at
the landing place, apparently to give her husband an honourable
reception. But just then, as Pompey took one of the crew's hand to

enable him to stand more easily, Septimius ran him through with his sword from behind . . .[10]

As Cornelia, distraught, gave the order to weigh anchor and escape, the assassins hacked off her husband's head and heaved his naked torso overboard, where it lay in a haze of blood and sand, lapped by the shallow waves. The head itself was carefully wrapped, a gift for the great Caesar when he came, a token of King Ptolemy XIII's loyalty, an offering (so it was calculated) to secure the powerful Roman's military support against the irksome Cleopatra. How wrong those calculations were.

And yet, how badly Caesar too miscalculated. When he arrived a few days later in the royal harbour at Alexandria, he caused a riot. In the words of his ghost-writer:

> As he was disembarking he heard a shout go up among the soldiers whom the king had left to garrison the town and saw a mob coming towards him. The reason was that the fasces [an axe held within a bundle of rods, tied with a scarlet thong, the symbol of a Roman magistrate's authority] was being carried ahead of him, which the crowd thought was a slight on the majesty of the king. The situation was calmed, but crowds kept gathering and rioting for several days on end, and not a few of Caesar's soldiers were killed throughout the city.[11]

To the Alexandrians, the coming of a Roman general with his war fleet and his legions, who then swaggered through their streets preceded by the hated symbols of imperial power, suggested the worst. Already, thanks to the Flautist, Egypt was in hock to Rome. Now, thanks to the weakness of the Flautist's son, it seemed that Rome's most powerful soldier had arrived in person to collect his dues.

Nor did Ptolemy's gift elicit from Caesar the reaction he and his advisors had anticipated. Instead,

> he turned away in loathing from the man who had come with Pompey's head, as if he were himself an assassin; and when he received Pompey's signet ring, with its engraving of a lion holding a sword in its paws, he burst into tears.[12]

Throughout his life, Pompey had modelled himself on Alexander the Great, even arranging his hair in the style of the Greek conqueror. Perhaps, gazing on his rival's face, Caesar reflected on the bitter irony of these men of Alexander's city gloating over Pompey's head, less than a mile from

where the embalmed, venerated and (so far) complete body of Pompey's hero, Alexander, lay in its mausoleum.

Whatever his musings, with such a reception, it did not take Caesar long to realize that there was something amiss in the kingdom of Egypt, and, given he had significant investments in the country (thanks to his financial relationship with its former king), he quickly decided that he was the man to sort things out. Citing Ptolemy the Flautist's wishes as expressed in his will that Rome should ensure stability in Egypt after his death, Caesar announced that he himself would mediate in person between the squabbling siblings, Cleopatra and Ptolemy XIII.

It was not the outcome which Ptolemy XIII had in mind. He was reluctant to accede to Caesar's demands that he present himself before him. Who did the Roman think he was to summon the Egyptian king as if he were some petulant boy? Still, for the moment, Ptolemy held all the cards, for he and his army were in control of Alexandria, the city where Caesar was now based, and to which he hoped to deny his sister access. For Ptolemy was determined that if he did not come before Caesar, neither would Cleopatra. Perhaps he was not ignorant of his sister's charms and her power to 'conquer everyone, even a love-tired cynic like Caesar, already past his prime'. Certainly he is likely to have heard of Caesar's reputation as a womanizer, a commander who would happily allow his troops, marching in triumph through the streets of Rome, to sing lustily of his sexual prowess.[13] So, aware of the possible human consequences of a meeting between general and queen, Ptolemy or his advisers were keen to do everything in their power to prevent it.

Yet their attempts were all in vain. Perhaps not yet in Alexandria, but elsewhere in Egypt Cleopatra enjoyed the support of her people. No doubt they appreciated that she had taken the trouble to learn their language; and early in her reign she seems to have gone to some lengths to show herself a willing devotee of their religion.

Three and a half years earlier, in 51 BC, in the city of Hermonthis in the Middle Kingdom, across the Nile just twelve miles south of Thebes, the so-called Buchis bull had died. This sacred creature, distinct with its white body and jet-black face, was thought to contain the spirit of the war god Menthu. In time, beside the temple complex, a cemetery had sprung up, the Bucheum, in which the mummified remains of generations of past bulls were buried, stretching back in an unbroken continuity to the times of the early pharaohs.

Only weeks after Ptolemy the Flautist's death, a new bull was to be installed and it appears that Cleopatra may have used the occasion to show herself to her new subjects. An inscription set up more than twenty years later records how the bull

The sacred Buchis bull, imbued with the spirit of the war god Menthu, receives an offering from Ptolemy II. Sandstone stele, 332 BC–30 BC, found at Hermonthis, Egypt. Height 56 cm; width 41 cm. British Museum, 1929,1016.164, donated by the Egypt Exploration Society.

reached Thebes, the place of installation, which came into existence aforetime, beside his father, Nun the old. He was installed by the king himself in the year 1, Phamenoth 19 [22 March 51 BC]. The Queen, the Lady of the Two Lands, the Father-loving Goddess, rowed him in the boat of Amen, together with all the barges of the king, all the inhabitants of Thebes and Hermonthis and the priests being with him. So he reached Hermonthis, his dwelling place . . .

Part of the inscription, 'he was installed by the king himself', is formulaic, but part is not, and the scene seems oddly plausible: the queen at the head of the flotilla, ceremonially rowing the tethered bull, its coat no doubt gleaming, its gilded horns glinting in the spring sun, upriver past lush fields (though, in the distance, arid cliffs and desert) to the sacred temple, where in three days time she would preside with white robed priests over the inauguration ceremony. Certainly Cleopatra kept a close relationship with Hermonthis throughout her reign, and the people of Middle and Upper Egypt seem to have stayed loyal to her.

Whatever prayers she had made to the war god Menthu at that ceremony three and a half years earlier, now in the bleak days of September 48 BC with Caesar in Alexandria and her brother trying to stop her reaching him, Cleopatra must have hoped they would be answered. Her solution to the blockade was typical both of her unconventionality and of the Ptolemaic love of theatre. For rather than risk the direct route either by land across the Delta where her brother's troops patrolled or by sea along the coast where his ships were lying in wait, she headed south with only a small retinue, perhaps to Memphis, the bustling pharaonic capital of the Old Kingdom, where the Nile divides.

It was here that the most perilous part of her journey began. There were but two of them: Cleopatra and one trusted officer, Apollodorus, a Sicilian.[14] In a small fishing boat, Apollodorus rowed the queen, disguised yet vulnerable, down the westernmost branch of the Delta, already, in the early autumn, blood-red with lotus flowers, the haunt of herons, ibises and egrets; and other creatures, too, Nile crocodiles and hippopotami, watched as they went. Perhaps it was before they entered Lake Mareotis that Cleopatra climbed into the canvas sack, to lie inert as the Sicilian manoeuvred the small boat through the canal which joined the lake to the western anchorage and then out, round Pharos island and so to the royal harbour, to the palace and to Caesar.

Perhaps he was expecting her; but even if he was, nothing could have prepared him for the drama of her entrance. The audacity of her appearance, smuggled in a sewn-up bag, appealed to him greatly. And Cleopatra had prepared well for her role: the vulnerable young woman lying at the great Caesar's feet, her clothing and her make-up no doubt calculated to achieve the perfect balance between Ptolemaic power and Egyptian exoticism, a promise of fecundity as enticing to the general as the great wheat-fields of the Nile. Caesar, the great conqueror, was conquered.

If there had been any doubt at all whose side Caesar would take, it vanished in that moment he set eyes on Cleopatra. How the interview proceeded has long been a seedbed for conjecture. The two would certainly have conversed in Greek. It was the queen's first language, and Caesar, like all educated Romans of his day, was fluent. No doubt he appreciated Cleopatra's turn of phrase, but this was probably not foremost in his thoughts.

The next day, when Ptolemy XIII, by now well aware of his sister's presence and all too eager now to meet his Roman visitor, was ushered through the palace for his audience with Caesar, it was already too late. For, seated in state in the throne-room next to the Roman general, flanked by legionaries and attended by palace courtiers, was Cleopatra, regal and triumphant. From their demeanour it was obvious to anyone they were already lovers. It was clear that for the moment, there was nothing Ptolemy could do. Swallowing his pride, he acquiesced to Caesar's orders. Cleopatra would be reinstated as the Queen of Egypt, ruling jointly with her brother. Their differences were to be put behind them. Their father's debt to Rome was to be paid.

Young Ptolemy responded by throwing the most spectacular royal tantrum, rushing from the palace and throwing his crown onto the pavement outside. It was only through the judicial use of force on the part of Caesar's soldiers that he was persuaded to return indoors. But his courtiers were not prepared to take their humiliation easily. Indeed, it seemed there was no need to. After all, even if their king was in enemy hands, their army had the royal palace surrounded; the rest of Alexandria was hostile to the foreign general; and with the autumn trade winds making it impossible for Caesar's fleet to put to sea, the Roman and his army of a mere two legions could go nowhere. Effectively they were besieged. No sooner did it seem that Cleopatra could congratulate herself for breaking her brother's blockade and reaching the protection of Caesar and his troops than the very place in which she had sought refuge had itself become fraught with danger. What she had hoped would be a haven had taken on the aspect of a war zone.

CHAPTER 3

Big City Blues

ALEXANDRIA: OCTOBER 48 BC

ALEXANDRIA WAS A CITY DIVIDED. Most of the town, including Pharos island, was controlled by Ptolemy XIII's general Achillas, while part of the palace complex together with the theatre was in the hands of Caesar and his legionaries. The odds were far from even. With Pharos in Egyptian hands, access through the narrow harbour mouth was well nigh impossible. Without such access, Caesar would be denied both supplies and reinforcements; and without these, he might in time be starved into submission.

Yet, Caesar was used to turning round difficult situations, and he did hold what he thought was one important card: the royal family, Ptolemy XIII, Cleopatra and her sister Arsinoë were all in the palace with him. This was useful both militarily and from a propaganda point of view. For he could claim he was protecting them from hostile insurgents, while, effectively, he was holding them hostage.

Caesar's first attempts to reach a settlement with the Egyptian army were far from promising. He put pressure on the boy king to send two senior negotiators to Achillas, but no sooner had they arrived in the Egyptian camp than they were set upon. One was killed, the other escaped seriously injured. Can we detect the hand of the Gabinian mercenaries in this brutal attack? Only two years earlier, Cleopatra had punished their colleagues for killing the two sons of a Roman consul, similarly on a diplomatic mission. Now, perhaps, they were taking their revenge.

Back in the palace, Caesar redoubled his guard on Ptolemy XIII and sat down to work out his options. Not only was he under siege, he was seriously outnumbered too. Had his two legions been at full strength, he would have commanded some 11,000 men. But they were not. Caesar might have had at most 10,000 troops at his disposal; the enemy had twice that number, as well as 2,000 cavalry. It must have seemed as if history was repeating itself. Seven years earlier, when he first invaded Britain (55 BC), Caesar had found himself similarly cut off, his ships destroyed in a storm,

A colossal granite statue of a late Ptolemy (116–87 BC) stands outside the modern Library of Alexandria. Found at Fort Qait Bey, Alexandria, Height 4.55 m. Alexandria Graeco-Roman Museum, 1001.

Above The late Roman Odeon (significantly smaller than the 1st century BC theatre) in Alexandria, 4th century AD.

Opposite A Roman galley under sail: silver *denarius* struck by Quintus Nasidius at a mint travelling with Sextus Pompey, 44–43 BC. (see p. 31 for obverse). Diam. 2 cm. British Museum, R.9115.

without his crucial cavalry, in an unknown hostile country. Through luck and perseverance he had saved the day. Would he be able to pull off a similar success again?

His first task was to reassure his men. The enemy, he told them, were nothing to be frightened of. Even the Gabinians (like them, trained Roman soldiers) had gone native,

> accustomed to the licentiousness of life in Alexandria. They had turned their back on the name and discipline of the Roman people, and had taken wives, by whom many had even fathered children. Alongside these men was a collection of brigands and pirates ... and many condemned criminals and exiles had joined them, too. Here at Alexandria all our runaway slaves could find safety and a guaranteed livelihood by enlisting in the army ... which even possessed an ancient privilege allowing it to demand the execution of the king's friends, to loot the property of the rich and to besiege the royal palace demanding pay rises.[15]

In short, he said, they were an untrained rabble. How he must have hoped that this was true.

Caesar's next task was to act. Quickly. The fleet of fifty warships, which

the Alexandrians had lent to Pompey, had recently returned. If Caesar's
men were to have any chance at all of gaining control of the harbour, it
was imperative that they should either requisition or destroy them. So,
with fighting raging across the city, and a sizeable detachment of his troops
involved in protecting the royal palace from attack, Caesar
sailed out into the harbour. His own account of what
happened next is frustratingly short, yet the outcome
was clearly not in doubt. By the end of the encounter
the enemy fleet, both the ships riding at anchor and
those in the dry docks, had been destroyed.

It was a signal victory. But mingled with the acrid
stench of smoke that gusted, cloying and heavy, in
the autumn winds across the harbour and the city and
the lake was another, even more disturbing scent, the
scandalous aroma of a cover-up. Like other great conspiracy
theories, it soon took hold. The charge was that the flames which
engulfed the Alexandrian fleet had spread, fanned by the wind, to engulf
and destroy the library. So says Plutarch; and so, too, Seneca, who adds that
40,000 books were lost that day. Writing in the second century AD, Aulus
Gellius confidently claims that the entire collection of 700,000 books was

> burned during the sack of the city . . . not intentionally or under
> orders, but accidentally by the auxiliaries.[16]

In many ways, Caesar is himself responsible, if not for the burning of
the library, then for the subsequent confusion. The brevity of his account
has suggested that he had something to hide, while early on in his (ghost-
written) *Alexandrian War* he makes the bold claim:

> Alexandria is virtually secure against fire; the buildings contain no
> joists or timber, and are all vaulted and roofed with rough-cast or
> stone tiles.[17]

Does he protest too much? As is so often the case, the truth is elusive,
but it seems increasingly unlikely that it was the great library itself that
burned. Instead, warehouses of books along the wharf-front may well
have caught light, with gossip and the love of a good story subsequently
exaggerating the extent of the disaster.

From a purely military point of view, the engagement for Caesar had
been thoroughly successful; and as the black pall from the harbour and the
dockyards engulfed the city, he disembarked his men on Pharos island. The
air thick with missiles, the Romans fought their way grimly forward until

they reached their goal: the lighthouse complex at the island's eastmost tip. Here, in the colonnades surrounding the great towering edifice, on the long vaulted ramp leading into it, up the broad spiral staircase climbing high into its heart, the fighting must have been the most ferocious. At last, though, Caesar's men won through, and by sunset, under the passive gaze of its marble statues of Zeus, Poseidon and a dynasty of Ptolemies, the Roman legionaries occupied the lighthouse and consolidated their control. Phase one of Caesar's plan had been successful.

Yet, he still could not afford to relax. Leaving others to organize affairs at the lighthouse, he returned with all haste to the palace. It was vital that as large an area of its grounds and buildings as possible should be fortified without delay, so Caesar recalled those troops which through the day had been engaged in inconclusive fighting in the city streets and set them to work building defences. By morning, a wall snaked through the palace gardens and up to the

> theatre adjacent to the residence, which served as a citadel and had access to the harbour and the dockyards as well. He augmented these defences on subsequent days, so that they could serve as a barrier in place of a wall, and he would not be obliged to fight against his will.[18]

For Cleopatra, no doubt watching anxiously from a window high up in the palace, the day must have been an education. If she had indeed led the regatta for the Buchis bull, she already knew the value of mingling with her subjects. But Caesar's single-minded and ferocious energy, throwing himself into the midst of battle, leading always from the front, staying up all night to supervise the building of the wall, cannot but have earned her respect and caused her to re-evaluate all that she thought she knew of leadership. Her emotions, too, must have swung wildly. By siding so emphatically with Caesar, she had already crossed her own personal Rubicon. It was essential to her own survival that he should win. Yet the sight of the royal fleet on fire, of the smoke engulfing the dockyards and seeming for a while perhaps to billow even from the library, of a foreign army occupying Alexandria's iconic lighthouse – all must have caused her to question (albeit briefly) where her allegiance lay, and maybe to conclude that, in matters of life and death, the ends justified the means.

When Caesar eventually returned to their quarters, his tunic streaked with sweat and stained with blood, his face and limbs all caked with ash and grime, he must have presented a sight which not only to the powdered eunuchs and the perfumed palace courtiers but to Cleopatra, too, was entirely alien. For Ptolemaic kings simply did not do battle in this way.

Despite being descended from one of Alexander's generals, they were much more content to pass control of fighting on to others, while they themselves got on with the ritual of governance. There must have been those in the palace who viewed the Roman and his troops with growing distrust.

One of these was Cleopatra's sister, Arsinoë. Perhaps she disliked what Caesar stood for; perhaps she was jealous of Cleopatra's flaunted relationship with the Roman general; perhaps she thought he could not win and that, if she made a move now, then she herself could become queen; whatever her reasoning, she managed somehow to evade the guards set up by Caesar and slipped out to join the besieging army and Achillas, their commander. Yet for Achillas, this was something he could well have done without. No sooner did Arsinoë arrive, than the two were quarrelling about how to wage the war.

Tantalizingly little is known about this 'other Ptolemy girl', Arsinoë. She is always in the shadow of her elder sister Cleopatra, her limelight stolen, her character impugned. Yet, had her fate been different, she might have proved an equally seductive subject for historians. No doubt educated to a similar standard as Cleopatra, she too may well have been a cultured linguist, a sparkling conversationalist, a mesmerizing beauty. Yet the jealous lens of time shows her as Cleopatra's unsuccessful, unattractive doppelgänger, a dowdy spinster doomed to make wrong choices, a spiteful sibling bent on ruining her sister's life.

Now with the forceful princess Arsinoë to contend with, the Egyptian general Achillas suffered another blow. For some time, it was said, he had been receiving secret intelligence reports from inside the palace. Their author was the eunuch Pothinus, tutor and regent to the young king Ptolemy. His agents were discovered and arrested. Pothinus was put to death. Perhaps Caesar was himself the executioner. Only weeks before, Pothinus had counselled Pompey's murder, an act Caesar claimed he abhorred. To kill the eunuch now must have been strangely satisfying. Besides, as Caesar later claimed, if he had not killed Pothinus, Pothinus surely would have tried to kill him.[19] In truth, whatever the real or trumped-up reason, it benefited Caesar to have the regent dead.

Outside the palace in the city, while Alexandria settled down for a protracted siege, its resourceful inhabitants (including, no doubt, the inmates of the museum) sought ever more innovative ways to bring it to an end. As more and more heavy artillery and missiles were brought in, shipped up the Nile, through canals and into Lake Mareotis from other parts of Egypt, whole areas of Alexandria itself resounded to the ceaseless din of hammering and sawing, while the streets and boulevards were barricaded in readiness for fighting.

They closed off every street and alley with a triple wall, built of squared blocks of stone and no less than twelve metres high, protecting the lower areas of the city with very tall towers, ten storeys in height. In addition, they had constructed mobile towers of equal height, with wheels and ropes, which could be towed by horses to wherever they were needed along the flat smooth streets.[20]

Caesar was clearly impressed. His reports speak of the 'intelligence and sharp-wittedness' of the Alexandrians, who, in addition to their own endeavours, quickly imitated whatever they saw the Romans doing and sought to outmanoeuvre them. He understood, too, just how high the stakes were for the Alexandrians. Not least because it was true, their message, 'if we do not drive [Rome] out, Egypt will become a province',[21] could prove a powerful rallying call, attracting increasing numbers to their cause and inciting their troops to ever more desperate acts of bravery.

But as so often happens, ego intervened. Ever since she had escaped from the palace, Arsinoë had been unhappy with her general, Achillas. Now she had him killed, appointing in his place as general his murderer, her tutor, the eunuch Ganymedes. As for Arsinoë herself, she held supreme command.

Ganymedes clearly was a clever man. No sooner had he assumed office than he put into practice a plan of potentially devastating proportions (though, whether he or Arsinoë had hatched it, we have no way of telling). He polluted Caesar's water supply. Sandwiched as it was between the desert and the sea, Alexandria relied for its fresh water on the Nile, and the city boasted an ingenious underground network of pipes, cisterns and filtration systems. The main channel as well as the spurs off it were now in the hands of the Egyptians, and, as Caesar explains, Ganymedes made the most of this fact:

> He blocked the water channels, isolating those parts of the city which he himself controlled; then, with the aid of water-wheels and other machinery, he pumped up vast quantities of water from the sea, and caused this to flow continuously down towards Caesar's part of the city. The result was that the water in the cisterns belonging to the nearest houses soon became saltier than usual . . . Before long, the water from this area was completely undrinkable, while that from lower down gradually became increasingly brackish and contaminated. This removed all doubt, and all the troops were seized with such fear that they thought themselves in the most extreme danger.[22]

Understandably so. Even in November, the temperatures in Alexandria are high, and without water the besieged Romans could not hope to survive for long. It might be possible, as Caesar knew, to ship in water from elsewhere, but that was not the point. Morale can be mercurial. It might not be long before discipline deteriorated and the legionaries demanded a hasty, messy and politically embarrassing evacuation. Caesar made a stirring speech and (no doubt with a heartfelt prayer to the goddess Luck) ordered his men to set about digging wells. 'Every coastal district', he informed them airily, 'naturally contains veins of fresh water.' Fortunately for him, this coastal district did, and, with their general almost certainly leading by example, they dug the night away – 'enthusiastically' according to Caesar's own report – until they found 'a great quantity of fresh water'.

The subsequent celebrations were matched only two days later when news came to the palace that help was on its way. The Thirty-Seventh legion, once part of Pompey's army, now loyal to Caesar, had put to shore some miles to the east, and with them they had food and weapons, missiles and heavy artillery. It was the answer to the besieged Romans' prayers. Yet there was a problem. The late autumn trade winds, which had prevented Caesar from leaving Alexandria, were now thwarting the Thirty-Seventh legion's attempts to reach him.

Or so Caesar claimed.[23] His subsequent actions suggest that this may not have been the only reason (or, indeed, the real reason) for their having anchored away from Alexandria. Caesar's typically vigorous response was to man his entire fleet and lead them out of harbour (while leaving his legionaries onshore to guard the palace and the lighthouse). Then he set on course to find the Thirty-Seventh. Perhaps Pompey's old legion was loath to enter a city already under siege. Certainly, had the trade winds really been an issue, Caesar never would have left harbour, as clearly he, too, would have been unable to return. For the Romans who remained in Alexandria, not to mention Cleopatra, that would have proved fatal. Something else, too, seems to be concealed in his account of the episode. The fact that he sailed with empty ships and did not make directly for the Thirty-Seventh but spent valuable time at anchor off the coast while his men went ashore to find fresh water suggests that his success in digging wells had not been quite so spectacular as his reports implied. A vital reason for his voyage was to fetch water.

It was now that Caesar's plans began to unravel. Unarmed, unprotected and preoccupied with filling the cumbersome water-skins, the shore party was ambushed by the Alexandrians and tortured. They quickly revealed that Caesar had no troops on board his ships. The Alexandrians could not believe their luck. As Caesar, with his own fleet now augmented with the warships and merchantmen of the Thirty-Seventh legion, tacked back towards the harbour mouth, he saw, dwarfed by the towering lighthouse and silhouetted against the evening sun, the Alexandrian navy. Despite the burning of so many of their ships, the Egyptians still retained a formidable fleet, and now it was waiting to give battle.

With night fast approaching, and reluctant to engage, Caesar ordered his ships to ride at anchor. But one of his vessels, at a distance from the rest, seemed to the Alexandrians an easy prey, and they attacked. Caesar had no option but to go to his vessel's aid, and, in the confusion of gathering darkness, his fleet captured one ship, sank another and inflicted heavy casualties all round. Demoralized, the Alexandrian fleet fled, and, in his own words,

> Caesar returned to Alexandria with his own victorious vessels, towing the merchant ships against a gentle breeze.[24]

Once more Caesar had turned a situation that (with hindsight) he should never have allowed to happen, into victory. Once more, too, Cleopatra learned at first hand a useful lesson in military command.

But the Alexandrians were far from beaten. Although Caesar had acquired new supplies, he now had significantly more mouths to feed. In addition, he and Cleopatra were still effectively besieged, and the Alexandrians calculated that, with a larger navy, they could reinforce the blockade and starve him into submission. So, they requisitioned as many vessels as they could find, including the customs boats that patrolled the mouths of the Nile delta, and set about repairing and equipping decommissioned hulks. With timber at a premium in tree-bare Egypt, they dismantled the rafters of porticoes and public buildings and planed them into oars. In an astonishing few days, they had assembled twenty-seven warships, as well as a number of smaller vessels, and were conducting trials of their new fleet in the western harbour.

In the palace, Caesar was growing impatient. The time, he felt, was fast approaching for the final showdown. Early one winter morning, his ships rowed out of the royal harbour mouth and round the tip of Pharos island to take up their positions. From the western harbour, as if in ritual reply, the newly refurbished Alexandrian fleet, too, issued forth. For a long uneasy moment, the two sides faced each other, motionless, neither prepared to make the first move for fear that they would end up grounded on the shoals which ran out from the island. Then, on Caesar's nod, four of his ships nudged forward. The battle had begun. Caesar's account is vivid. It tells of skilful helmsmanship, as Roman vessels were manoeuvred head to head against their Alexandrian attackers, always looking for a way to slice in close, to cut them up and sheer off their banks of oars. It tells of blazing missiles, ships locked tight together in the narrow strait; of fierce and bloody fighting from the decks; of all the rooftops in the city crammed with people, Romans and Alexandrians alike, all straining hard to watch, and among them surely (though he does not name her) Cleopatra. But at last, Caesar's fleet prevailed. The Alexandrians turned tail and rowed in desperation back to the safety of their harbour, while, from the shore, their comrades pelted the pursuing Romans with a rain of missiles.

Just as before, when he had burned the Alexandrian fleet, Caesar was not content to leave things there. Rather, he knew that now was the time to press home his advantage. Although the lighthouse was his, the rest of Pharos island, together with the Heptastadion causeway linking it to the mainland, remained in enemy control. What better time to seize them than when the Alexandrians were in such disarray? So, rapidly transferring into tenders and small dinghies, he rowed round to attack the island from the harbour side, while his navy assaulted it from the sea. For a while, the islanders resisted, firing from the rooftops of houses and from the many towers, some ten metres tall, which clustered round the settlement. But then panic set in. Many dived into the sea and tried to swim across the harbour to the safety of the city. Some made it; most did not. By nightfall, Caesar claims that he had taken some 6,000 prisoners.[25]

Caesar, his head crowned with laurel, is shown as 'Dictator Perpetuus' ('for life'). Silver *denarius*, Rome, 44 BC. Diam. 2 cm. British Museum, 1843,0116.170.

With darkness came looting and a lull in fighting, but the dawn saw Caesar once more in full armour, his purple cloak slung from his shoulders, at the head of a flotilla of small boats heading for the Heptastadion and that part of Pharos island nearest it, which was still under the Alexandrians' control. A savage hail of arrows soon turned the islanders to flight, and as some of the Roman soldiers jumped ashore to clear such pockets of resistance as remained, others ran down the Heptastadion to a point where it could best be barricaded. On the causeway they hurried to throw up a wall; beneath it they worked hard to fill with stones and try to block the archways through which boats could sail from one harbour to the other.

For a while, all went to plan. But then, somehow unseen, a number of Alexandrian troops appeared behind the Romans on the causeway, between the barricade and Pharos island. As reinforcements joined them, it was the turn of many of the Romans, including some of the oarsmen who had left their boats to help, to feel the chill of panic. In confusion, they leapt from the causeway into the small boats, some trying to pull in the gangplanks while others still struggled to get on board. By the barricade, Caesar tried in vain to rally his troops, but in the end even he had to concede that it was a lost cause. Maintaining as much order as he could, he retreated to his boat, but even here he was not safe. As more and more men began to pile on board, the boat sank dangerously lower in the water. Fearing the inevitable, Caesar shrugged off his purple cloak and leapt into the water to swim across the harbour to where his warships rode at anchor. Many of his men were not so lucky. Hands grabbed frantically at sides of boats, terrified men tried to haul themselves on board, and, overwhelmed by numbers, one by one the tiny vessels sank. The Alexandrians, victorious, poured out across the Heptastadion and back onto the island, which they overran and fortified, installing ballistic missiles and taking control of the harbour mouth.

As ever, there was perhaps more to this encounter than Caesar would later admit. With his boats sinking round him, we hear of a curious detail:

> Caesar leapt off the causeway into a small boat and attempted to go to the assistance of his men. But the Egyptians swarmed around him on all sides, so he dived into the sea and swam to safety, albeit with difficulty. It is said that in his hand he was clutching many papers which he would not let go, even though he was in the water and being fired at constantly, but he held them out of the water in one hand while he swam with the other. His little boat sank shortly after he left it.[26]

What were these papers, which Caesar was so desperate to save? Did he rescue them from the sinking boat, or did he have them with him all the time? What would have been the implications of their loss? They were clearly of vital importance if Caesar was prepared (as is clear from later accounts) to risk his life for them. Yet, like so much in this story, all that this episode can do is help to illustrate the gaps in our knowledge and counsel us to beware of becoming complacent.

The situation had reached stalemate. In the streets of Alexandria, the ten-storey-tall wheeled towers still rumbled daily through the boulevards in search of weak spots in Caesar's defence, while in the palace, richer by the day with the unaccustomed reek of unwashed Roman soldiery, the tempers of the royal household must have been reaching breaking point. The behaviour of young Ptolemy XIII, impotently sitting on his jewel-encrusted throne, a royal hostage prone to tantrums, is not recorded. But in the weeks following the debacle at the Heptastadion, Caesar seems to have felt significant relief when a delegation from the Alexandrians arrived requesting that he release their king to them. They had had enough of 'the harsh dictatorship of Ganymedes', they complained.

Caesar, motivated (in his own words) 'not by generosity but by shrewd calculation', readily gave in to their appeals. He later wrote that he suspected there was more to their requests than met the eye, for 'he was very well aware that this was a deceitful nation, always given to dissimulating their real intentions'. If so, they had met their match, for Caesar knew that, with

Ptolemy XIII in their camp, the Alexandrians would soon find themselves the unwilling spectators of a spectacular show of sibling rivalry and bitter jockeying for power. Arsinoë, for one, would not relish the arrival of her petulant younger brother. How Cleopatra reacted to seeing him go is a matter for speculation. Certainly the boy's departure from the palace was dramatic. Perhaps with Cleopatra at his side, Caesar

> took him by the hand and began to dismiss this boy who was nearly an adult. But the king (who, like the rest of his race, was an expert in deceit) started weeping and begging Caesar not to send him away. Not even his own kingdom, he said, was dearer to him than Caesar's company. Caesar was himself moved, and drying the boy's tears, he assured him that, if those were indeed his sentiments, they would soon be reunited.

In fact, they were *not* his sentiments. In the next sentence, Caesar writes:

> [Ptolemy], like a beast released to freedom from its cage, began to conduct the war against Caesar so fiercely that it became apparent that those tears he had shed at their parting had been tears of joy.[21]

And so the situation might have dragged on. But by now, in 47 BC, help was on its way to the beleaguered Roman army. Now that spring had come, Mithridates of Pergamum was marching to their rescue. By sea, too, ships laden with supplies were lumbering south, hugging the coast of Syria, soon to reach Egypt. The Alexandrians were dismayed. They stationed warships at the sacred pleasure town, Canopus, to try to intercept the Roman fleet. Caesar sent his own ships to attack them; they were beaten off.

Yet soon news came to Alexandria that Mithridates and his men had reached Pelusium, the frontier town, the eastern gate to Egypt, that he had overrun it, and that he was camped close to the Delta. In haste, the Alexandrian army, mustered on the banks of Lake Mareotis, began without delay to board the river boats and barges which had been gathered there. With oars ruffling the glassy surface of the shallow lake, Ptolemy XIII, Ganymedes at his side, and maybe, too, Arsinoë, led the Egyptians out into the network of canals and streams, and then onto the Nile and to the eastern Delta.

It was the moment Caesar had been waiting for. The long months of cramped street fighting and indecisive skirmishes were over. At last there was the chance for a proper pitched battle. Leaving a few men to guard the palace, he embarked his troops and sailed out of the harbour, past Canopus on his right with its great temple of Serapis, and past Herakleion, and so entered the Nile.

Already, by the time that Caesar's troops found Ptolemy, he had received good news. Wishing, no doubt, to do battle before Caesar could arrive, Ptolemy's advance guard had attacked Mithridates' camp. But their discipline had been poor. Mithridates' men had easily defeated them. Now, though, the Egyptian king had taken up position on a well-defended hill, protected on one side by a marsh, and on another by the Nile itself. Yet rather than wait to be attacked, when Caesar was still seven miles away Ptolemy sent all his cavalry as well as some light infantry to intercept him. For the Romans, so long cooped up in Alexandria, this must have seemed like a gift from the gods. Their repressed frustrations exploded in a welter of blood-lust against the Egyptian troops. Hacking through any opposition, Caesar's men pressed on until they came to Ptolemy's encampment.

Rather than attack that day, Caesar insisted that his forces rest, but with the dawn came the last battle. While long-range missiles rained down on the Egyptian camp, the Romans found their way in. As Ptolemy's men ran down to the ramparts to defend them, Caesar could see that they had left the hill-top largely undefended. He sent a cohort in to take it. Now, attacked both from below and from above, the Alexandrians

> terrified by the noise of fighting coming from both sides, began running about their camp in disarray. Our own [i.e. Caesar's] men, heartened by this panic, entered the camp from all sides almost at the same time. Those running down from the higher ground slaughtered a great number of the enemy in the camp. A great many Alexandrians, in their attempt to escape from danger, threw themselves in droves from the rampart on the side next to the river ... It is agreed that Ptolemy himself managed to escape from the camp and was taken on board a ship; but because of the large numbers swimming for the nearest ships, the vessel was waterlogged and he drowned.[28]

Caesar gave orders to retrieve the body. It was important that no one should believe the king still lived. Yet all that was found was his golden armour. The boy himself had vanished in the Nile.

The war was over. As the victorious Caesar approached Alexandria, he found himself mobbed by crowds of citizens, many dressed in ritual robes of supplication, among them shaven priests presenting the most sacred objects from the city temples, all appealing to the general to show them clemency. With a theatrical display of magnanimity, he did. He accepted their submission, and, to the resounding cheers of his own troops, he made his way back through the city to the palace, and to Cleopatra.

Peace may have come to Egypt, but elsewhere throughout the Roman Empire there were still those who supported Pompey's cause. In Africa and Spain there was still campaigning to be done. Yet Caesar showed no haste to leave. For a little while, no doubt, he could have argued that he wished to give his men time off from fighting. The siege, coming as it did hot on the heels of Pharsalus and the battles that preceded it, had patently exhausted everyone. There could be no harm in stopping for a week or so. But a week became a month, and it soon became clear that Caesar had other plans.

For a cerebral man like him, the museum must have held a certain interest. The library, as well, if its books were not all blackened from the fire, offered unique opportunities to peruse early editions of philosophers and poets. Then there were scientists and architects, astronomers and engineers whose expertise might be profitably harnessed back in Rome. But most of all, there was Cleopatra, now undisputed queen of Egypt and, as importantly for Caesar, soon to be the mother of his child.

Cleopatra had her own plans for Caesar. For generations, a visit to the sacred crocodiles and a quick trip up the Nile had been de rigueur for celebrated foreign visitors. Now, however, with the Roman world's most powerful man to entertain, Cleopatra arranged a cruise more ambitious in its scale and lavish in its execution than any the ancient land of Egypt had ever seen. Written evidence of the cruise is scarce. Caesar himself

'A seductive promise of infinite fecundity': the River Nile flows past the mountains of the Western Desert, north of Aswan.

does not mention it, which suggests that, while he was clearly happy to go along with it, it was not part of his own master plan. The historian Appian accords it one disapproving sentence:

> He cruised down the Nile with 400 ships to view the country in the company of Cleopatra, and he took pleasure with her in other ways as well.[29]

Modern authors have made much more of it. Certainly, given her Ptolemaic pedigree (as well as her subsequent spectacular stagings) Cleopatra is likely to have ensured that this would be a voyage to remember. And not just for Caesar, but for her subjects, the Egyptians, too. Nor would it be a simple pleasure cruise, but rather a hard-headed show of her authority.

If, in her adolescence, she had appreciated the powerful symbolism of the journey to Hermonthis with the Buchis bull, now, as an adult queen, already showing the signs of pregnancy, Cleopatra knew the deep importance of this voyage. For now it was not a sacred bull that shared her barge, but Caesar himself. For all the numinous and otherworldly strength believed to reside in the bullock of Hermonthis, it was nothing compared to the naked power of Rome and the authority of its human representative. News of Ptolemy's defeat and death must have travelled upriver before her. If any of Cleopatra's subjects still thought to resist her, the sight of Caesar and of the barges lined with Caesar's men would give them pause.

Egypt meets Rome: the remains of a Roman-period Temple of Isis (foreground) are dwarfed by the pyramids at Giza.

Yet, the voyage was more than a show of power. As the flotilla pushed further south, the breathtaking fertility, the infinite fecundity of Egypt revealed itself in all its seductive promise. Undoubtedly the pyramids impressed, and the labyrinth by Lake Moeris. So too the temple at Luxor by the Nile at Thebes, with its colonnade of sphinxes leading off to Karnak, while, beyond, giant statues, thirteen metres tall, stood by the desert's edge at the entrance to the Valley of the Kings. So too the temple of Isis, the island sanctuary at Philae and the sacred crocodiles. But, for Caesar, always mindful of the mouths of Rome, these were but baubles compared to the richness of the soil and the lushness of the riverbanks.

So, as they sailed south, Cleopatra unashamedly laid out her country, naked and unguarded, before Caesar. He had the power (as he had shown already) to seize it all by force. How much more useful, though, if he were coaxed into a partnership. How much more valuable for Egypt and for Cleopatra if Rome bought, rather than took by force.

In June came Akhet, the annual Nile flood, and as the waters rose the pleasure boats returned to Alexandria. The deal was done. Caesar confirmed Cleopatra queen of Egypt. She had (he later wrote) 'stayed loyal and remained under his protectorate'.[30] Of course, she had to marry her young brother, Ptolemy XIV; but he was only thirteen, a mere figurehead. For Arsinoë, their sister, however, Caesar had other plans. She, after all, had fought against not only him but Rome, and, as a captive leader, she would be sent back to the empire's capital in chains.

In the form of a crocodile, the god Sobek wears an Atef crown. Bronze statuette made in Egypt around 600 BC. Height 12.5 cm; length 10 cm. British Museum, 1902,1013.4.

For now, though, Caesar had other business to attend to. An eastern war loomed. It was time to go. Leaving two legions behind at Alexandria, he said his farewells to Cleopatra, now only weeks away from giving birth, and with his fleet behind him, sailed out past Pharos lighthouse for the final time. When he and Cleopatra met next, it would be in Rome.

CHAPTER 4

The Desperate Hours

ROME: SEPTEMBER/OCTOBER 46 BC

CLEOPATRA'S YOUNGER SISTER may have reached Rome first, but if she did, it was in circumstances very different to those of Cleopatra's own arrival. For while Arsinoë, who had for a few months reigned as queen of Egypt, was brought to Rome a captive, Cleopatra entered the city as the honoured guest of its most powerful man, the father of her infant son, the victorious general, Julius Caesar.

Unlike the geometrically planned Alexandria, Rome was a messy maze of twisting alleyways, where rich villas nestled beside temples, aqueducts jostled for their place near crowded squares and a sprawl of shops, bars and slums spread out haphazardly across its seven hills. Once there, the royal Egyptian retinue took up its residence across the River Tiber from the city proper, in Trastevere, in one of Caesar's leafy villas. Caesar himself was living elsewhere with his wife, and the dwelling he had chosen for his guests was sufficiently detached to ward off scandal, but close enough to town to allow for easy contact.

It may not have been Cleopatra's first taste of the imperial capital. Nine years before, in 55 BC, she may have accompanied her father, Ptolemy the Flautist, in his exile to Rome. If she did, she would, ironically, have stayed in the villa (famously adorned with the beaks of captured warships) of her lover Caesar's greatest rival, her father's patron Pompey.

Now in 46 BC, however, Cleopatra was accompanied not only by her young husband-brother, Ptolemy XIV, but by her son (later to be named Ptolemy Caesar, but now called by the Alexandrians 'Caesarion'). With her, too, was a vast menagerie of courtiers and attendants, priests and advisers, eunuch civil servants, dressers, maids, perhaps some eggheads prised from the museum and (without doubt) a high-powered trade delegation.

Egypt had come to Rome, but to define the exact nature of the relationship between the two superpowers must have required some skilful negotiation, if not tight-rope walking. Suetonius tells us that Caesar summoned Cleopatra to the city, but not the reason why.[31] It is unlikely

Imperial Capital: the Roman Forum, looking eastwards from the Sacred Way below the Capitoline Hill towards the (later) Colosseum.

59

to have been for purely sentimental reasons. Even though Caesar had no other son, and openly acknowledged his paternity of Cleopatra's child, Roman law would not allow Caesarion to be his heir. Nor would it have been entirely politic for the Roman general to parade too openly his relationship with the Egyptian queen.

Elephants pull a chariot in which Jupiter rides in triumph, crowned by winged Victory. Silver *denarius*, Rome, 125 BC. Diam. 1.65 cm. British Museum, 1904,0204.36.

Rather, Caesar may have wished to return the compliment which Cleopatra had paid him eighteen months earlier. Then, he had been shown the wealth of Egypt. Now he would demonstrate to Cleopatra the power of Rome. Cleopatra's first visit as Egyptian queen to the heart of the Roman Empire may even have been timed to coincide with perhaps the greatest demonstration of pure naked strength which the city or its leading citizen was ever to present: four triumphs in the space of a few days; four processions through the streets of Rome to celebrate four victories over four ancient powerful nations. What made the occasion so ambivalent for Cleopatra was that one of those nations was Egypt.

If any in the Alexandrian entourage ensconced beyond the Tiber was in doubt as to what a triumph meant, Caesar's house-slaves would no doubt have happily informed them. It was, they would have learned, an ancient, ever-changing institution, which dated back, so some believed, to the foundation of the city itself. It celebrated both a victory over subjugated peoples, and the general who had won it. It brought the captives and the spoils of war into the very heart of Rome, paraded as they were before the chariot in which the general was carried, with the clash of hobnail boots on paving stones resounding as his legions strutted haughtily behind him. As the procession snaked its way towards the Capitol, the religious heart of empire, where the temple of Jupiter Maximus Optimus (the Greatest and the Best) towered over the city, its course was lined with spectators, some watching from specially built grandstands, most marvelling at this clear demonstration of the undisputed power of Rome. What made these triumphs of their master, Caesar, special was that there were so many of them and that they marked his domination of three continents: Europe, Asia and Africa.

The first of the triumphs, on 21 September 46 BC, marked Caesar's conquest of Gaul and his victories in Britain. If the general had waited six years for this day, so had the defeated Gaulish leader, the imposing Vercingetorix, who would now be led in chains in front of Caesar's chariot. With his stronghold at Alesia facing starvation, Vercingetorix had been forced to surrender to the besieging Romans in 52 BC. Ever since, he had been kept in prison in anticipation of these final hours.

Despite the ritual humiliation Vercingetorix was forced to suffer, he must have experienced one moment of wry satisfaction. During the procession

> Caesar endured a bad omen. When he reached the Temple of Good Fortune, the axle of his triumphal chariot broke, and he had to complete the remainder of the procession in another vehicle.[32]

For the intensely superstitious Romans, this was serious indeed. Fifteen years earlier, Pompey, too, had been forced to abandon his triumphal chariot. Admittedly, on that occasion it was because the event organizers had failed to do their homework. To maximize its impact, Pompey had arranged for his chariot to be drawn by elephants. When they tried to pass beneath an arch they got stuck, and Pompey had to transfer to a more conventional mode of transport. At least that spoke of merely human error. An axle breaking opposite the Temple of Good Fortune could be seen to suggest that a divine hand was at work.

The remainder of the triumph went off without a hitch. From his new, intact chariot, drawn by four white horses, Caesar could see ahead of him the ranks of captives, many carried, crouched in chains, on biers, borne shoulder high so that the crowds could view them. Interspersed with these were wagons bearing images of towns that he had taken, forts he had destroyed, models, perhaps, or paintings. Massive placards were carried high displaying the names of conquered cities and the grim statistics of the war: a million Gauls killed, another million enslaved. As the triumphant general descended from his chariot to climb on his knees in ritual obeisance up the steps of the temple on the Capitol, Vercingetorix was led away and strangled.

Whether Cleopatra saw the triumph with her own eyes or merely heard reports from those who had, we do not know. Nor can we fully imagine her feelings as she anticipated the second of the processions a few days later. This was to be Caesar's triumph over Egypt, his celebration of his victory in the war at Alexandria. For a domestic audience at Rome, this triumph must have held a great appeal. It was a chance for them to see at close quarters the exotic wonders of a far-off land. It validated, too, the long months Caesar had spent on the Nile. But for the Alexandrians themselves, and Cleopatra most of all, things were much less clear cut. Caesar had, they might have argued, fought on one side of what had been an Egyptian civil war. He had confirmed the legitimate ruler, Cleopatra, on her throne. He had been entertained by her and shown great hospitality. Egypt remained, in name at least, an independent nation. Perhaps it was for this reason that the historian Appian referred to this procession as 'a *kind* of triumph'.

61

What, then, was paraded through the streets on this occasion? Not plunder, surely. It is unlikely that Caesar had stripped the royal palace or the museum or the library at Alexandria, or any of the ancient sites of Egypt of their wealth. Perhaps such monies as were carted through the streets were Ptolemy the Flautist's loans repaid, though there are no records of even these being on display. Instead, we hear of wagons carrying a statue of the Nile as river god and a model of the Pharos lighthouse, complete with fire and flames, items which might perhaps suggest that Caesar used this triumph to demonstrate the ingenuity of the inventors housed in the museum, counterparts of other more far-reaching innovations he was seeking even now to introduce from Alexandria to Rome.

But people and prisoners played their part as well. As the trumpets blared, crowds cheered the effigies of the dead Achillas and the slaughtered Pothinus, while paraded before Caesar's four white horses may have been Ganymedes, the defeated leader of the Alexandrians, who had once tried to pollute the palace water.[33] Yet it was not the eunuch general who drew the people's gaze. It was Arsinoë. And the presence of this woman, this mirror image of the enigmatic and alluring Cleopatra, disturbed them.

> The sight of Arsinoë, a woman honoured as a queen, in chains – something never yet before seen, in Rome at any rate – aroused enormous pity.[34]

It was not the reaction Caesar had anticipated. Even if the boisterous verses of his triumphant legions, as they sang their saucy songs about his love for Cleopatra, faded from Rome's memory, the sour note struck by the sight of the captive queen would be difficult to erase. After the triumph, Arsinoë was freed from her chains and sent to Ephesus to serve in the celebrated temple of Artemis (like the lighthouse in her native Alexandria, a wonder of the ancient world). Yet even here her brooding presence would be felt, her rivalry of Cleopatra never sated.

By 2 October, the quartet of triumphs was complete. In the third, to mark his swift victory in the war over Pontus, for which Caesar had set out on leaving Alexandria in 48 BC, the general famously caused one placard to be borne aloft proclaiming his success in three short words: *veni, vidi, vici* (I came, I saw, I conquered). In the fourth triumph, for his subsequent war in Africa, where he had mopped up many of the remaining followers of Pompey (47–46 BC), he exhibited not only the infant son of the enemy king Juba, but

> twenty diverse pictures portraying all that had happened, as well as the people involved. Only Pompey was absent. Him alone he chose

not to show, since the people still missed him greatly. Though cowed, the crowd groaned as they saw the disasters suffered by their own people, and especially when they saw [a depiction of] Lucius Scipio, the commander-in-chief, stabbing himself in the chest and throwing himself into the sea, Petreius committing suicide at his banquet, and Cato tearing himself open like a wild beast.[35]

It was not only parades that marked these extraordinary eleven days in the early autumn of 46 BC. Lavish banquets were held, too, with hand-outs to the city poor, while the rich were fed on lampreys washed down with the finest wine.[36] Plays were produced in a variety of languages, performances of pseudo-ancient Trojan games were staged and money was showered liberally upon veterans and civilians alike. As Caesar's biographer Suetonius, with access to the imperial records, wrote:

> Wild-beast hunts were held for five days in a row, and the performance was rounded off with a battle between two armies, each with 500 infantry, twenty elephants and thirty cavalry. Caesar had the central barrier of the Circus, around which the chariots raced, removed to enable the two camps to be sited opposite each other. A temporary stadium on the Campus Martius was erected for three days of athletic games to be held. On an artificial lake . . . a sea battle was fought between heavily manned Tyrian and Egyptian ships, with two, three or four banks of oars. So vast were the numbers of visitors who flocked to these spectacles from every direction that many were forced to sleep in tents set up in the streets, or on roofs; often the sheer pressure of the crowd caused people to be crushed to death.[37]

With the huge numbers of prisoners and captives slain in the arena and of animals sacrificed or hunted in the Games, the days of Caesar's triumphs were an orgy of death. Yet, they ended with the dedication in his gleaming new Forum of a temple to Venus Genetrix (Venus the Begetter), the goddess from whom his family claimed descent.

> After dinner on the last day [of the triumphs], Caesar entered his own Forum wearing slippers and garlanded with all kinds of flowers; from here he returned to his house escorted by almost the entire populace – as well as by many elephants carrying torches . . . Now, having completed his new Forum and the temple to Venus (the founder of his family), he held a service of dedication, and inaugurated many contests of all kinds in their honour.[38]

The Temple of Venus Genetrix in Caesar's Forum (dedicated 46 BC) contained a statue believed by many to represent Cleopatra.

Inside the temple he erected a statue, which in time would become controversial. As one second-century AD historian commented: 'Beside the statue of Venus he placed a beautiful statue of Cleopatra, which still stands there today.' Another wrote: '[Cleopatra's] jewels are now dedicated in our temples, and a gold statue of the queen herself can be seen in the Temple of Venus.'[39] The statue was probably not of Cleopatra at all, but rather the Egyptian goddess Isis, associated in the Romans' minds with Venus, but the fact that Cleopatra portrayed herself as the embodiment of Isis encouraged the confusion. Not even Caesar would have had the gall to bestow divine status on a living foreign woman in a temple in the heart of Rome. To populate a Roman shrine with Egyptian gods was revolutionary enough. However, the image of Cleopatra did appear to have a major impact on fashion in Rome, her hairstyle being imitated by wealthy ladies of the city.

Yet it was not just animals to be sacrificed or captives to be killed or statues to be dedicated in his temple that Caesar had brought back from Alexandria to the relatively old-fashioned Rome. He had brought back ideas, too, and now he worked feverishly to turn them into new realities, circumventing or ignoring the conservative Roman senate with all the monomaniacal energy that had characterized his military campaigns.

'When in Rome': a marble portrait, probably from Italy, c.50–30 BC, shows Cleopatra VII in a distinctly Roman style. Height 27 cm. Staatliche Museen zu Berlin, Antikensammlung, Berlin, 1976.10.

The year 46 BC itself was the subject of reform. It was to last 445 days. Rome's calendar had become spectacularly out of kilter. For centuries it had been based on a lunar cycle of 355 days, with extra months being introduced as necessary to keep it more or less in step with the seasons. The problem was that, with the recent upheavals of the civil wars, no one had bothered with these extra months, so the calendar was inaccurate by some eighty days. Now Caesar took the opportunity to amend things once and for all. With the help of the astronomer Sosigenes, one of the experts from the Alexandrian museum who had accompanied Cleopatra's Egyptian delegation, Caesar imposed on Rome the calendar of 365-and-a-quarter days that remains in use today. In addition, and with equally lasting effect, he renamed his birth-month 'July'.

Nor was this the only way in which he sought to bring Egyptian influence to Rome. Haunted perhaps by the reek of burning manuscripts which wafted from the warehouses of Alexandria, on his return from that city he had already commissioned the building of 'the finest public libraries, commissioning Marcus Varro to collect and classify Greek and Latin volumes'.[40] Rome might not have possessed wide, shaded and sophisticated boulevards, but it would have books.

Canals, too, started to be dug. In Egypt, Caesar must have gazed in admiration at the network of man-made waterways that spider-webbed out from the Nile. Now back in Italy he proposed the digging of a channel to the Tiber that would drain the Pontine Marshes, malarial swampland south of Rome, and reclaim the land for agriculture. For Greece, his plans were more ambitious still: a canal would be dug through the rocky isthmus close to Corinth to facilitate sea travel through to Athens and beyond.

For many of the Romans it was too bewildering. The pace of change was moving far too fast. For a time, however, neither Cleopatra nor Caesar himself were around to experience the discontent which the reforms provoked. By late November 46 BC, Caesar had already set out on campaign again, this time to Spain and the last bastion of Pompey's sympathizers. By then, too, Cleopatra and her great Egyptian entourage may also have left Rome, to chance the winter sea-lanes back to Alexandria.

Much had changed in the two years since she had smuggled herself at night into the palace at Alexandria in her canvas bag. Then, Cleopatra's hold on power had been tenuous to say the least. Now it was vice-like. In the few months since the Alexandrian War had ended, she had not simply promoted people she could trust into the top jobs, but must also have cracked down ruthlessly on any opposition. Had Egypt not been so secure, she never could have risked so many crucial months in far-off Rome.

Nor was it only the political face of Alexandria that had perhaps been changed. As the royal fleet rowed with pomp and ceremony into the great harbour for festivities to mark their queen's triumphant return from Rome, Cleopatra herself may have scanned the waterfront, impatient to see how her major new building project was progressing. For (according, at least, to the Byzantine chronicler Malalas), before he had left on campaign, Caesar himself had begun work on a huge new complex which in time would come to dominate the Alexandrian skyline. The Caesareum was:

vast and of the wondrous beauty, being situated opposite the best harbour; nothing like it can be seen in any other city, so full is it of offerings, pictures and statues, and decorated as it is all round with silver and gold. Its precinct is of great breadth, adorned with porticoes, libraries, men's banqueting halls, groves, gateways, spacious courts, open-air rooms: everything, in short, with which lavish expenditure could embellish it – its very sight affording confidence to voyagers as they enter or leave the harbour.[41]

Isis suckles the baby Horus, a representation favoured by Cleopatra to bolster her own image after the birth of Caesarion. Terracotta, 1st century BC. Height 7.4 cm. British Museum, 1938,0314.1, donated by George Davis Hornblower.

Situated as it was between the theatre and the Museum, it is possible that the Caesareum was rising from the ashes of those very buildings burnt in the late autumn firestorm two years earlier. Although it was still clad in scaffolding, the statement it already made must have been deeply compelling. For here was a demonstration in marble of the union between Cleopatra, Egypt's queen, and Caesar, the first man of Rome. Here was an indication of their bond, as unequivocal and as insistent as their son Caesarion himself, already eighteen months old and learning his first words.

Indeed, the image of Caesarion, soon to enjoy the title 'Lover of his Father', was already being used exquisitely to bolster his mother Cleopatra's image. Now that she had an infant at her breast, the queen could truly take her place in Egypt's heart as the human incarnation of the mother-goddess Isis, so often pictured suckling or cradling or dandling on her knee her son, the deathless Horus. Just as in Rome the Isis statue took the character of Cleopatra, in Egypt Cleopatra merged more closely with the goddess.

In time, at Dendera in Upper Egypt, giant reliefs of Cleopatra and Caesarion would be carved onto the shrine of Hathor, the goddess who had served as Horus' wet-nurse, while just to the south at the great cult centre of Hermonthis, where even now the white-robed priests were polishing the gold horns of the Buchis bull, an elegant birth temple would rise to be reflected in the waters of the Nile. As a subsequent description tells us:

> [Caesarion's] birth is realistically depicted alongside that of the God Horus ... Cleopatra is shown kneeling attended by goddesses, and above her is her new name 'Mother of Ra (the Sun-god)' in hieroglyphs. Over the new-born child stands symbolically, the device of the scarab [sacred beetle], marking out the young Ptolemy Caesar as God of the Rising Sun. On a couch apart sit two cow-headed goddesses suckling two infants, clearly the young god Horus and the young Caesarion. In addition, not only the god Amon and the goddess Mut but also Cleopatra herself are shown appearing on the scene in response to the joyful event.[42]

The influence of Cleopatra?: Limestone head of a woman resembling Cleopatra. Made in Italy, c.50–40 BC. Height 28 cm. British Museum, 1879,0712.15.

Not only now in 46 BC but in the turbulent years ahead, Cleopatra invested much in her young son. To her people, the Egyptians, he was one of their own, the child god Horus who, along with Isis and Osiris, formed their holy trinity. To the Romans, he was the father-loving son of Caesar, the general who had saved Cleopatra in the past, whose troops now kept her firmly on her throne, and who, she must have hoped, would continue to protect her in the future. The queen had made her choice, and publicly. She had thrown in her lot with Caesar.

Within a year, communicating almost certainly by letters borne on slow ships plying their sluggish journeys between Spain (where Caesar was campaigning) and Cleopatra's Egypt, she made arrangements to return to him in Rome. Again, the visit is unlikely to have been purely social. For one thing, with the last vestige of support for Pompey well and truly squashed, Caesar was already planning a campaign east to Parthia to win back the eagles lost by his erstwhile colleague Crassus. For such an undertaking, a reliable supply-line was essential, and what better source of grain, ships, men or money than nearby Egypt?

Yet, already in Rome tongues were wagging and the rumour mill, so active in the city's chicly introverted, self-important salons, was producing ever more fantastic gossip. Even the magnificent excess of Caesar's Spanish triumph in October 45 BC was in danger of being overshadowed by speculation fuelled by the exotic presence once more across the Tiber of the Egyptian court. Since his return from the East a year or so before, Caesar seemed hell-bent on recreating Rome in the sophisticated image of Alexandria. Now, with Cleopatra a seemingly permanent fixture whenever Caesar was in Rome, his critics went so far as to accuse him of thinking of transferring the capital of his empire to her Egypt. Or perhaps to Troy. No one really knew.

None of this stopped many of the great and good of Rome from climbing into their best litters and ordering their slaves to transport them across the river to Trastevere and an audience with the Egyptian queen. One such was Cicero, the pompous lawyer-politician who still liked boasting to anyone foolish enough to listen of how he single-handedly saved Rome from dictatorship some seventeen years earlier. Perhaps he embarked on some such tale with Cleopatra. He certainly failed to make the mark he felt that he deserved. Later he wrote of how

> I cannot but be outraged when I think of the queen's impudence, when she was resident in Caesar's house in his gardens in Trastevere.[43]

Others were indignant, too, and word began to circulate not only that Caesar meant to make Cleopatra his wife, but that he was intent on proposing a law to allow him to marry as many wives as he wished for the purpose of begetting children.[44] Both rumours were absurd in the extreme, but they serve to illustrate the frenetic mood of the time.

No less frenetic, but much more sinister and all-pervasive, was the speculation that Caesar intended to have himself proclaimed king. For many, the very idea was abhorrent. They relished the fact that since the heroic Lucius Junius Brutus had driven Tarquin the Proud into exile in 509 BC, no king had ruled the city for over 450 years. Instead, in the resultant republic, a complex system of balances had been put in place, where power was in the hands not only of the senate but of the Peoples' Tribunes, and where the government was headed by two consuls. Now, though, many feared that the old order was slipping. Caesar's autocratic and impatient style was all very well on the battlefield, but in domestic politics it could be abrasive.

As preparations for the campaign east to Parthia grew in momentum, so did the rumours. Some pointed to Caesar's propensity for being seen at all times resplendent in the purple robes of a triumphing general, his head wreathed with a crown of laurel. Others spoke incessantly of how, in the senate house, he now sat on a golden throne, of how his statue stood in line beside those of the ancient kings, of how a ceremonial chariot and litter carried Caesar's effigy in ceremonials around the hippodrome. It was as if he thought himself an Eastern king – it was as if he were a Ptolemy – and it did not help that he was seen to be consorting with a Ptolemaic queen.

As the date of his departure for the Parthian War drew ever closer, people started to speak out more and more. Voices on the street began to address Caesar as 'king'. A laurel wreath bound in regal white ribbons was placed on his statue's head, and verses were daubed on his statue's base, reading:

> Caesar sent the consuls on their way,
> So Caesar reigns as king today.[45]

In fact, the poem was premature. There were still consuls. Caesar was one of them. But his colleague in office, rather than challenging him, appeared not only to be supporting Caesar in his ambitions but positively pressurizing him to become king. At the Lupercalia, a festival held annually in mid-February to promote fertility, the behaviour of Caesar's fellow consul stoked the flames the more.

> The consul tried several times to crown Caesar as he was addressing the crowd from the Rostra [the speakers' platform in the Roman Forum]. But each time Caesar refused and in the end he sent the crown to be dedicated to Capitoline Jupiter.[46]

While all this was going on, with just over a month left before Caesar's departure for Parthia, Rome must have been experiencing a flurry of activity as last-minute arrangements were being made and checked. In Trastevere across the Tiber, too, crates were undoubtedly being packed as the Egyptian court made preparations to return to Alexandria, for with Caesar gone, there was no longer any reason for Cleopatra to stay in Rome. Her leaving was no doubt scheduled to coincide with Caesar's.

Meanwhile, the mood among many of Rome's senators became increasingly bleak. Speculation grew that one of their number was intending to use a conveniently discovered prophecy (that Parthia could be defeated only by a king) to hasten Caesar's elevation. As the days slipped past, they found themselves faced with an appalling dilemma: to risk letting Caesar accrue even greater glory for himself in Parthia (where, on the other hand, he might equally well suffer ignominious defeat like the unfortunate Crassus) or take matters into their own hands and put a stop to him before he went. They chose the latter course.

On 15 March 44 BC, three days before he was due to set out on campaign, Caesar attended a meeting of the senate, held not in the Senate House itself, but in a sprawling complex of recreational and business facilities built by his erstwhile rival and called Pompey's Theatre. Later, people all too readily remembered omens of disaster, and even on the day itself there were those who sought to stop Caesar from attending. Yet, mid-morning, Caesar entered the assembly room.

> As soon as Caesar sat down, the conspirators pressed around him as if they wished to pay their respects. When Tillius Cimber, who was in the front, came close by him, as if to ask a question, Caesar signalled to him to wait, but Cimber took hold of Caesar by the shoulders. Caesar exclaimed, 'this is outrageous!' and turned away. But at that very moment, one of the Casca brothers slashed at Caesar with his dagger and stabbed him beneath his throat. Caesar grasped Casca's arm, stabbed it with his stylus, and jumped back. But a second dagger blow stopped him. Faced as he was by a ring of drawn daggers, he covered his face with the top of his toga, unbelting the lower part, and allowing it fall to his feet so that his legs might be decently covered when he died. He was stabbed twenty-three times, but did not make a sound after Casca's first attack had made him groan; but there are some who say that when he saw Marcus Brutus poised to strike the second blow, he rebuked him in Greek saying, 'Even you, my son?' All the senators then scattered in confusion, leaving Caesar lying there dead ... [47]

Moralists could not resist the perfect symmetry of the image of the dying Caesar, sprawled in an empty hall built by his greatest rival,

> against the plinth on which stood Pompey's statue. The plinth was so steeped in Caesar's blood, that one might have imagined that Pompey himself was presiding over this act of vengeance on his enemy, who now was lying prostrate at his feet, his body quivering from all his wounds.[48]

As news rippled out from Pompey's Theatre, a ghastly numbness shrouded Rome. No one knew who next would feel the edge of the assassins' knives. For all that day and the next night, all who had been of Caesar's circle hid behind locked, barricaded doors, listening for any sound that might suggest approaching danger.

For the Egyptians, trapped in the dead man's villa in Trastevere, the long hours must have felt desperate indeed, caught as they were between an urge to stay, safe in the house, and an overwhelming urgency to leave. Everything that Cleopatra had battled hard to build had in a few swift dagger strokes been overthrown. Only that morning she had woken secure in the knowledge that she had the backing of the strongest man in Rome. Now, with his death, her future and that of Egypt were in sudden jeopardy. For who could tell how Caesar's enemies would treat his erstwhile friends? Who could know how the assassins would view Caesar's only son? To escape from Rome was vital, to reach Egypt fast essential.

Yet, even as the Ptolemaic party slipped out of the city unopposed and boarded the ships which would convey them home, news must have begun to reach them that already Caesar's fellow consul was beginning to take charge, that he was rallying the Roman people and persuading them not to abandon everything that Caesar had once stood for. Perhaps all was not lost. Perhaps this fellow consul was an ally. If, as they discussed him on their journey home, there were those among Cleopatra's entourage who could not recall the consul's name, they would soon have no such trouble. It was Mark Antony.

'Ides of March': Gold *aureus* of Marcus Iunius Brutus, celebrating Caesar's assassination in 44 BC. Struck in 43–42 BC at a mint travelling with Brutus. British Museum, coin on loan from Michael L. J. Winckless.

CHAPTER 5

Conflict

ALEXANDRIA: LATE SPRING 44 BC

IN ALEXANDRIA, with its love of spectacle, return of the royal Egyptian fleet from Rome must have bestowed excuse enough for carnival. A mere eighteen or so months earlier, when her galleys had rowed into the royal harbour, the queen could tell her people in all honesty that everything was well. Now, as the late spring of 44 BC unfolded into early summer, Cleopatra had to play an altogether different game. Despite her own fears and misgivings, it was essential that she reassure her people, that she present a calm unruffled face to Alexandria, that she scotch once and for all such rumours as might run wild in the streets that, in relying too heavily on the now dead Caesar, she had made a grim and perhaps fatal error.

At least Cleopatra was alive. There may have been times between Caesar's death and her arrival home in Alexandria when her own fate hung in the balance. Back in Rome, news had reached a delighted Cicero suggesting that all was not well with Cleopatra. On 11 May, he wrote spitefully to a friend: 'I hope the news about the queen and that Caesar [i.e. Caesarion] is true'.[49] Frustratingly, he does not reveal what the news actually was. Only days later (17 May) Cleopatra was again the subject of Cicero's stylus, when he observed that 'the rumour about the queen is dying down'; but a week later (24 May) he was still maliciously 'hoping that it is true about the queen'.[50] Again, just what the rumour was, we do not know. His gleeful tone suggests he hoped she might have met her death, perhaps in childbirth, perhaps in shipwreck.

If rumours such as these reached Rome, they must have been rife in Alexandria as well. All the more reason for the queen to stage a confident return. Yet, behind the scenes, she cannot but have worried as she waited, hungry for news from Rome, determined to play her part in the newly re-ordered world as constructively and positively as she could.

She must certainly have placed some hope in Antony. As the aftermath of Caesar's murder brought his fellow-consul Antony into ever-sharper focus, Cleopatra would without doubt have been reminded how, as a

The spirit of Caesar lives on: part of a basalt statue, possibly showing Caesarion, c.35–30 BC. Said to be from Karnak. Egyptian Museum, Cairo, 13/3/15/3.

young and dashing cavalry officer, Antony had ensured that the return of her father, Ptolemy the Flautist, from exile back to Alexandria was accompanied by the maximum stability and the minimum bloodshed (see below). At that time, eleven years before (55 BC), his had been a safe pair of hands. Now, he seemed again to be the right man for the job.

Perhaps Cleopatra had still been barricaded in the villa, across the Tiber from the hubbub and the threat of Rome, when, three days after Caesar's murder and the uneasy stand-off which had followed it, Antony convened a meeting of the Senate (17 March). Here, he proposed that rather than seek vengeance, an accommodation should be reached with the assassins to ensure a lasting peace. Not only this. He succeeded, too, in gaining the senators' approval to ratify all of the dead Caesar's acts and decisions, including those which had not yet been implemented. It was a move which must have won the wily Cleopatra's admiration. Because Antony had possession of all Caesar's papers, he effectively controlled the legislation.

Three days later, his charismatic power was on display once more, but this time to a wider audience (20 March 44 BC). It was the date set for Caesar's public funeral, and Antony intended to exploit it to the full. For centuries, the death of a leading politician had been marked by elaborate obsequies and ritual: processions and speeches praising his achievements and placing him squarely within the panoply of Roman heroes. Historians traced the tradition back 400 years, to the ceremony held (ironically enough) in honour of Lucius Junius Brutus, the founder of the Republic, and ancestor of one of Caesar's assassins.[51]

Curiously, although others among the (still distinctly subdued) assassins objected to Antony's demands that Caesar should have a public funeral, their colleague, the present Brutus, was not one of them. Rather, he backed Antony when he insisted

> that [Caesar's] will should be read out in public, and that the body should not be buried secretly or without the proper honours, in case this too should antagonize the people.[52]

The stage was left wide open for Antony's creative instincts to run riot. So, with an eye to the spectacular (worthy of the best Alexandrian impresario), he did his best to ensure that Caesar's funeral rites would be not only moving but theatrical, a presentation of hard-headed, hard-hitting political propaganda wrapped in a seamless shroud of well-choreographed mass mourning.

The *mise-en-scène* had already been artfully prepared. As productions of tragedies carefully chosen 'to raise pity and indignation for his murder' were being staged throughout the city, a gilded model of Caesar's temple to Venus Genetrix (Venus the Begetter, see p. 64)

> was set up before the Rostra [Speaker's Platform], and inside it an ivory couch, draped in purple and cloth of gold. At the head was a trophy, on which was hung the [blood-stained] toga in which he had been killed.[53]

Meanwhile, from outside the city walls to the west, from the flat-lands of the Campus Martius a solemn procession wound its way towards the Forum. At its heart were the highest magistrates of Rome, their heads veiled ritually in mourning, bearing on their shoulders the bier on which lay Caesar's mutilated corpse. All around, musicians filled the air with wails and dirges.

When they reached the heart of the city, the body on its bier was set down on the Speaker's Platform, high above the Forum with its vast and teeming ocean of so many countless faces stretching back as far as any eye could see, expectant, nervous, focused, until at last, into the swell of such anticipation, Antony himself strode out to take his place: on cue, and centre stage.

No one recorded his exact words. Many have tried to recreate them. If (as is likely) his speech followed convention, he would have listed Caesar's many achievements, how he had striven for the greater good of Rome, how he had loved its people. Using tellingly theatrical vocabulary, one account describes how Antony

> swept up his clothes like a man possessed by a god, and fastened them with a belt so that his hands were free. Then, standing next to the bier, as if he were on stage, he stooped low and, restrained at first, chanted praise to Caesar as if to a heavenly god, stretching up his hands in witness of Caesar's divine birth while at the same time rattling off the list of his wars, his battles and his victories, as well as the nations he had brought under Rome's rule, and the spoils he had sent home.[54]

The effect upon the crowd was palpable. Antony already had them in the palm of his hand. Now, like the instinctive showman that he was, he could not stop himself from ratcheting up their emotion still further.

> Carried away by passion, he stripped Caesar's body and raised up his clothes on a spear, brandishing them, torn and ripped as they were by daggers and stained with the dictator's blood. At this, the people, like a chorus, lamented with him with great wailing and from sorrow they were again consumed by anger. The funeral speech over, other lamentations and funeral songs were performed over the dead

according to the Roman tradition by choruses, which again recited his achievements and his fate.

But even this was by way of a mere overture. The explosive *coup de théâtre* was yet to come. Here was the climax of the whole extravagant production, a scene stolen unashamedly from the conventions of Greek tragedy:

> When the crowd was in this emotional turmoil and very close to violence, someone raised above the bier a wax effigy of Caesar (the actual body itself was lying on its back on the bier and so could not be seen). The effigy was rotated in every direction by a mechanism to reveal the twenty-three wounds to his face and body – a truly horrific sight.

On stage, this was an ancient and well-used device. Many Greek tragedies had ended with a hero or a god suspended high above the audience, a technique known as *deus ex machina*, sometimes resolving conflicts, sometimes giving dire predictions for the future. The device which Antony now used seems so much more sophisticated, a successor to those clever hydraulic mechanisms used to such significant effect in processions staged on the streets of Alexandria. Perhaps it had even been built for him by those same Egyptian experts whom Caesar had summoned to Rome as part of Cleopatra's entourage.

By now, emotions were running so high that not even Antony could control the crowd.

> That was the end of any orderly procedure; people shouted 'kill the murderers', while others . . . dragged benches and tables from shops, and piled them up, creating a huge pyre; on top of this they laid Caesar's body, and surrounded by so many sacred and inviolate shrines, they burned it.[55]

The imperial biographer Suetonius adds:

> Then the flute players and professional mourners removed the robes they were wearing – robes which had been previously worn in Caesar's triumphs – tore them apart and cast them into the flames, while Caesar's veterans threw in their ceremonial armour, which they had worn to mark his funeral. A large number of married women, too, offered up their jewellery, together with their childrens' tunics and bullae [amulets worn by young children]. A large number of foreigners joined in this great outpouring of public grief, each lamenting according to their native customs.[56]

While all this was going on in the Forum, elsewhere on the streets the tension pent-up in the week since Caesar's death erupted into violence. Gangs of men ran through the alleyways, making for the houses of those known to have been part of the conspiracy. They found them empty. Brutus, Cassius and the rest had seen the future and had fled.

But Antony had seen the future, too. In the days before the funeral, he had read out Caesar's will. Much was as might have been expected: hand-outs to the citizens; the gardens of his villa in Trastevere, the house where Cleopatra and her court had lodged, left as a gift to the Roman People. But there was one surprise and its consequences were to resonate for centuries. Caesar had named as his heir not Antony, as might perhaps have been expected, nor even his own infant son Caesarion, which, as his mother was Egyptian, would have been illegal. Instead, he had named his nephew, an infirm, sickly youth of barely nineteen years, with no significant achievements in either politics or war, a boy still training overseas in Apollonia (in modern Albania), whose only real experience of public life had been to organize the pseudo-ancient Games two years before: Octavius.

What Octavius lacked in maturity and background, he made up for in ruthlessness, determination and self-belief. No sooner had he heard of Caesar's death and the contents of his will than he hastened back from Apollonia to Rome to claim his new inheritance. He found the city changed beyond all recognition. With Caesar dead and the assassins gone, Antony was de facto in control. Octavius and he may each have enjoyed a close relationship with Caesar while he lived, but now he was dead there was little love lost between them. In fact, quite the opposite.

From the start, Antony had been the antithesis of Octavian. Born (like Cleopatra) into an ancient patrician family riddled with debt, Antony had devoted his early youth to 'dissipated living' on such a scale that he himself soon owed his creditors the eye-watering sum of 250 talents.[57] In an attempt to default on this debt, he had fled to Greece, where he

gave himself over to military training and to the study of oratory, where he favoured the so-called Asiatic style, which was then at the

Charismatic and creative: Mark Antony (probably) represented in a green basalt bust, c.40–30 BC. Probably from Canopus, near Alexandria. Height 42 cm. The National Trust, Kingston Lacy, The Bankes Collection.

height of its popularity, and had many similarities with Antony's own character, which was boastful, hot-headed and full of empty arrogance and inconsistent bravado.[58]

The lessons, which would culminate in his funeral speech for Caesar, were already eagerly being learned.

It was in Athens that Antony attracted the eye of the general Aulus Gabinius, who invited him to serve on his expedition to Syria and Egypt in 55 BC: their mission to return Cleopatra's father, Ptolemy the Flautist, to the throne. In the resulting struggle, not only Antony's bravery, but also his compassion, became legendary:

> As soon as Ptolemy entered Pelusium, he was so consumed by his anger and hatred that he was about to massacre the Egyptians, but Antony intervened and stopped him. In the many hard-fought battles which followed, Antony was noted for many acts of bravery and for wise leadership . . . As a result, he left behind him a glowing reputation among the Alexandrians, while his fellow Romans on the campaign considered him a most outstanding man.

So outstanding, in fact, that he soon found himself summoned to serve Caesar (54 BC). He did so with great verve, first in a military role in Gaul, and then in a political capacity in Rome itself, where he was entrusted with promoting and defending Caesar's interests in the Senate. When civil war erupted, he served as both the regional commander of Italy and, at the decisive battle of Pharsalus, where Pompey was defeated, as the general in charge of Caesar's crucial right wing (48 BC).

While war had promoted Antony to the first ranks, peace was to prove less generous. With Caesar still on campaign in Africa (47 BC), Antony was once more entrusted with the command of Italy. It was disastrous.

> His easy-going nature led him to ignore those who had been wronged; he became irritable whenever anyone approached him for help; and he acquired a bad reputation for having affairs with other men's wives.

The bond between Antony and Caesar was stretched to breaking point. The crunch came over a rich house in Rome, which Antony had appropriated as part of his share in the spoils of war. When Caesar insisted he should pay the market price for it, the two men quarrelled and Antony was forcibly removed from public office. With hindsight, the subject of their quarrel could not have been more telling, for the house in question had once belonged to Pompey. It was none other than the villa (its hall adorned with the beaks of captured warships) in which Ptolemy the Flautist, and perhaps his daughter Cleopatra, had lived during their period of exile from Egypt.

Following his squabble with Caesar, Antony's years in the political wilderness were dogged by scandal. The moralist Plutarch, writing some four generations later and drawing on what were undoubtedly hostile contemporary reports, writes of how his fellow citizens

> were disgusted at his unseasonable drunkenness, his squandering extravagant sums of money, his debauches with women, his days spent sleeping or wandering about hungover or still drunk, his nights passed at parties or at shows or at the wedding feast of some mime artist or comedian.

He tells of how, after a night of partying, Antony vomited one morning in the Forum 'into his toga, which one of his friends held ready for him', of how he travelled Italy openly accompanied by one of Rome's most notorious actresses, of how he indulged in every excess possible. What shocked the austere, moralistic Romans most of all was Antony's love of 'luxuria', a term which smacked of Eastern decadence, louche living, and that pernicious seductiveness which, unleashed, might undermine all the Republic stood for. Looked at another way, this 'luxuria' was the epitome of Alexandria's hedonistic underbelly. Strip away the censorious spin, and Antony's festivities are oddly similar to those of Ptolemy II Philadelphus, two hundred years before (see pp. 16ff.):

> People were outraged at the sight of the golden wine cups which accompanied him (as if for some religious procession) in his trips out of the city; at the tents which were pitched on these journeys, at the sumptuous banquets laid out in orchards or on riverbanks; at his chariots drawn by lions; at his requisitioning of decent men and women's homes to house prostitutes and sambuca-players.[59]

It seemed that Antony already had about him something of Dionysus, the god so beloved of Eastern monarchy.

In time, Caesar and Antony were reconciled, and on 1 January 44 BC, the two men took on their new roles as joint consuls. A mere seventy-three days later, Caesar was dead. Whether Antony had known of the assassination in advance has been debated ever since. Certainly, he was conveniently removed from the scene before the knives were drawn, but whether this was to stop him trying to save Caesar or to ensure he was not implicated will forever be a matter of conjecture.

What was certain was that the world had changed dramatically. Just four years after one bloody civil war had ended, another seemed to loom. For Cleopatra, devouring the latest intelligence reports from Rome or Greece or Asia, the weeks and months that followed her return to Alexandria must have been troublesome indeed. She had experienced at first hand how a Roman civil war could spill over into Egypt. She had already heard how greedy eyes had lustfully devoured the spectacle of the Egyptian triumph. She had herself already seen in Rome how interested its insatiably rich speculators were in Egypt's harvests. She must do all she could to shore up her own power.

By August her brother, co-ruler and potential rival, Ptolemy XIV, was dead. If the cause of the fifteen-year-old's death was (and remains) unknown, its timing played magnificently into Cleopatra's hands – to such an extent that many found it difficult not to credit her with some involvement in it. For, with her sibling gone, the kingly throne of the Ptolemies fell vacant, and by now the sole male member of the dynasty who still survived to occupy it was Caesarion. On 2 September 44 BC, this child of Caesar and Cleopatra, now only three years old, was proclaimed the King of Egypt.

No records survive of the magnificence of his coronation, but no doubt the waterways, which rippled out from Alexandria east to Herakleion and to the rising sun, were crowded with well-wishers as the royal party made its scented, flower-strewn way towards the temple where for generations the Ptolemies were crowned. No doubt, too, along the Nile, in temples strung like jewels south from Memphis to Thebes to Hermonthis and Philae, prayers rose, thick with incense, for the boy-king's reign.

At last, by accident or by design, Cleopatra was effectively sole ruler of her country. Yet, even as she was giving her royal assent to the growing numbers of statues and sculptures now sprouting up across her peaceful fertile land depicting her as the goddess Isis, her young son Horus at her breast, she must have been all too aware that, even if the lands within her borders were secure, events unfolding rapidly elsewhere could easily wreck all that she had worked for.

When, with the coming of the spring (43 BC), the sea lanes opened once again, the news which trickled into Alexandria from Rome and Italy must have been worrying indeed. Already the fissures formed at Caesar's death had turned first into cracks, then chasms. While Egypt was celebrating Caesarion's coronation, in Rome Antony's most bitter rival, the insincere and fawning Cicero, began to unleash a campaign of vitriol against him. When Antony led out an army against one of the assassins, who had illegally refused to give up control of his province, the Roman stage was set for turmoil.

The atmosphere was dangerous enough, but what made it worse was the presence of Caesar's heir, Octavius. For the boy had proved everybody wrong. Sickly he may have been, but he was far from being a fool. Showing a brilliant grasp of Roman politics, he had won the Senate over to his side, and now, backed gleefully by Cicero, he had been granted the supreme military command, *imperium*. At the same time, thanks to back-room deals and calculated promises, Antony's opponents had engineered an edict proclaiming him an enemy of the state. Now, with the full force of the law behind him, Octavian (as he was now known) rode out from Rome at the head of his massed troops: his mission, to attack not Caesar's assassin who was still clinging onto his command, but Antony.

By the time that spring was giving way to a scorching Egyptian summer, it must have been increasingly difficult for those in Alexandria to form a clear idea of just what was going on in far-off Italy. Ships arriving in the harbour may have set off from the west some days apart, and the news brought on one might contradict that brought on others. But which to believe? Events were moving so rapidly, and, like the desert just a few miles from the Ptolemaic palace, the truth must have seemed as unformed as the shifting sands.

As Cleopatra's advisers verified reports, they would have learned that by April 43 BC in northern Italy, the armies of Octavian and Antony had twice met in bitter battle, once at Forum Gallorum and again at Mutina (modern Modena), and both times the more experienced Antony had been defeated. Now Antony had fled across the Alps and it seemed as if his days were numbered. But just as the Alexandrian diplomatic elite were consigning Antony to history and considering, none too hastily perhaps, the wording of their letters of congratulation to Octavian, the kaleidoscope of Roman politics shifted once again.

Now the news was that two of Caesar's assassins, Marcus Junius Brutus and Gaius Cassius, were gathering an army. Their intention: to march on Rome. No doubt the court at Alexandria must have cursed the coming of the autumn, when the sea became more turbulent and messages must travel much more slowly, for by now intelligence was filtering through that affairs in Italy had taken a new, unexpected course. By November 43 BC, the unthinkable had happened. Together with a third man, Marcus Lepidus, the enemies Octavian and Antony had met on an island in the River Po at

Young, cold and ruthless, Octavian positions himself as the heir to Caesar. Marble head from a statue, probably c.30–25 BC. Height 35.5 cm. British Museum, 1888,1012.1, donated by Rev. Greville John Chester.

Bologna, and with their armies drawn up on either riverbank, had carved out a treaty.

The so-called Second Triumvirate may have been as uneasy an alliance as the earlier relationship between Caesar, Pompey and Crassus had been, but this time it was official. Known now as *Triumviri Rei Publicae Constituendae Consulari Potestate* (the Triumvirs with Consular Power to Save the Republic), the three men were, in fact, invested with dictatorial authority. They wasted no time in using it.

Now that it was clear that battle lines had been drawn up between the triumvirs and Caesar's assassins (whose stated goal, of course, had also been to save the dying Republic); now that the Roman world was about to be plunged once more into a costly civil war, the two sides scrabbled frantically for money. For the triumvirs, the solution was not only clear but also chillingly ruthless. It had Octavian's fingerprints all over it. Proscription lists were drawn up containing the names of any rich Roman who in some way was an enemy of the triumvirs. Indeed, some were not even enemies. What mattered was that they were rich, for all were to be killed, their fortunes confiscated.

The personification of Libertas (Freedom): gold *aureus* of Gaius Cassius Longinus. Roman, struck in 43–42 BC. Diam. 2.1 cm. British Museum, 1855,0512.39.

With the death squads stalking the plush villas of Rome and the leafy lanes of prosperous Italian estates, news of the fate of one man at least may have brought a smile to Cleopatra's painted lips. Cicero, vindictive letter-writer, bumptious orator, had been intercepted as he swithered over whether to escape. In an act of uncharacteristic heroism, he had offered his neck meekly to the executioner's blade. His head was sent to Rome, his vituperative tongue to be gleefully pricked by needles; his severed bloodless hands were nailed to the great doors of the Senate House. Within a few brutal weeks, the triumvir's coffers were bulging, Octavian had the money he required for war and Antony's personal financial problems were at an end.

Closer to Alexandria, however, in the Eastern Mediterranean were the forces of Caesar's assassins, Brutus and Cassius, and they, too, needed money. Naturally they turned their sights on fertile Egypt. Bit by bit the situation Cleopatra had most feared was beginning to become reality: the storm clouds were gathering; a Roman civil war was brewing; once more Egypt was being drawn inexorably in; and once more its very independence was being threatened.

Whose side, then, should Cleopatra take? Geography might suggest that of Brutus and Cassius, whose troops were uncomfortably near to Cleopatra's territories. On the other hand, these were the men who had murdered her son's father. She surely could feel little warmth for them. As for Octavian, however, Caesar's heir, what hope was there that he would clasp his cousin Caesarion, the one true son of Caesar, to his bosom in familial love? Precious little, surely. Of Lepidus, the Alexandrians knew not a lot, so it must have been on Antony, if anyone, the officer who had once spared their country from vengeful bloodshed, that any hopes were pinned. And even Antony's track record had, of late, failed to convince. In his two most recent battles (against Octavian) he had been beaten. Better perhaps to support neither side too openly. Better perhaps to sit on the fence.

But this was not to be an option. With the assassin Cassius already occupying Syria, Cleopatra sent four legions out against him. But instead of fighting, they surrendered, leaving Syria in Cassius' hands and Cleopatra open to the charge of aiding Caesar's murderers. She quickly tried to redeem herself. When Cassius sent envoys to her, demanding food and

Cleopatra and Caesarion (third and fourth from the left) make offerings to the gods on the south wall of the Temple of Hathor at Dendera. 50–40 BC.

money, she prevaricated, citing as excuse poor harvests. Meanwhile, at the head of the Egyptian fleet, she set sail in her flagship north for Greece, in support of the vast army Octavian and Antony were massing there. She had learned from Caesar the importance of a leader being seen to lead in person. Now she would put that lesson to the test.

Or so she thought. The weather, though, put paid to all her plans; Cleopatra and her ships were driven back to Alexandria and the war went on without her. She made no further efforts to set sail. Instead, throughout the long, hot, agonizing summer of 42 BC, she and her courtiers played a waiting game, watching the horizon for ships which might bring news from Greece, while hoping against hope that there would come no message from Pelusium that Cassius' army had crossed into Egypt. There was at least one heart-stopping moment. Cleopatra's man in Cyprus had declared for the assassins, and rumour had it that he was in secret negotiation with Arsinoë, her sister, still in exile up in Ephesus (see p. 62). The whisper was he was addressing her as 'queen'; the implication, that if the assassins won, Cleopatra and Caesarion would be swiftly and ruthlessly despatched from their thrones.

With early autumn, the quaysides at Alexandria were again abuzz with rumour. Reports had come in from northern Greece that the two sides had at last met. The plain at Philippi was crawling with armed men – as many as 95,000 legionaries and 13,000 cavalry in Octavian and Antony's army facing 85,000 legionaries and 20,000 cavalry in that of Brutus and Cassius; more than 200,000 fighting men in all, and in their life or death hung the fate not only of the Roman world, but of Egypt too.

All Alexandria could do was wait. For days, there was no news. Nothing conclusive, at any rate. There had been skirmishes, but little more. Octavian was ill. It seemed that siege-works were being built and trenches dug. At last (3 October 43 BC), a battle; heavy fighting; stalemate; Cassius had killed himself. There followed no news for two weeks or more, the sea becoming choppy, until, just when it seemed that nothing would be settled, reports arrived at Alexandria of the decisive battle. On 23 October, the two sides had clashed. Such was the sheer weight of their numbers that the encounter turned into a messy disarray:

> There was little use for the usual volleys of arrows, rocks or javelins, since they did not use any strategy or technique. Rather they came to close quarters, their swords drawn, hacking and hacked, trying to break through the enemy ranks ... At last Octavian's troops ... began to push back the enemy line, as if they were overturning a massive piece of heavy machinery. Step by step, the enemy were pushed back, slowly at first and still showing determination; but in time their ranks

began to break, and now they gave way more quickly, and as those in the second and third lines joined in the retreat they all became confused in disarray as they were crushed not only by their own men but by the enemy, who did not let up until it became a rout.[60]

The next day, Brutus too was dead. The war was over, the triumvirs had won, and Cleopatra could once more make her plans.

In the aftermath of Caesar's killing, events had taken on a breakneck speed all of their own. Now, two and a half years later, it was time to take stock. Already, Octavian, Lepidus and Antony had carved up the world they had won at Philippi. Octavian was to control the west; Lepidus, Sicily and Africa; while Antony would have the east; and so it was in Athens, one of the most ancient capitals of his new domain and the city in which he had already passed so many pleasant months as a young student of oratory, that Antony chose to spend the Roman world's first winter of its hard-won peace. Here, in the violet shadow of the Parthenon, he charmed the Greeks with his urbanity and wit, while all the time he made plans for the future.

There was much that needed to be done. Among the vexingly unfinished business, carried over from a decade or so earlier, was the fate of Crassus' eagle standards, captured so disgracefully in his defeat in Parthia (see p. 34). For the sake of Rome's honour, they must be regained, and to regain them, Antony must lead an expedition east. First, though, he must ensure that his new provinces were loyal, and, to do that, he must visit every major city in its turn, win over those he could by generosity and charm, and punish those who could not be won over.

In the spring of 41 BC, Antony began his progress, first east to Asia Minor and then south along the azure coast to its dazzlingly wealthy cities, whose names had resonated through the centuries as bywords for luxury. For a man who had begun his life in crippling debt, it must have been a fantasy come true, and, always the showman, Antony was determined to travel in style. He was aware of the potency of the god Dionysus in the hearts of the peoples of the East, and knew, no doubt, of their processions for the god, processions like that staged by Ptolemy II Philadelphus in the hippodrome at Alexandria two centuries or so before.

Now, Antony would go one better. He himself would play the part of Dionysus. But Dionysus was a complex god. Concealed behind his smiling, hedonistic and benign exterior was a cruel, malicious heart. As any Greek or Roman who had seen performances of *Bacchae* by Euripides must know, Dionysus was as capable of acts of vengeance as he was of kindness. In fact, Rome's ancient enemy the Parthians knew, too – it had been, after all, in a staging of that drama that Crassus' severed head had played a starring role (see p. 34).

Now Antony played Dionysus with panache.

> All Asia was thick with incense . . . When Antony made his entry into
> Ephesus, women dressed as Bacchants, with men and boys costumed
> as Satyrs and Pans led the procession. The city was hung with ivy,
> bristling with thyrsuses and loud with the music of psalteries and
> syrinxes and flutes, while the people greeted him as Dionysus the
> Beneficent, the Bringer of Joy. There is no doubt that this was how
> some people thought of him, but to most he was Dionysus, the
> Flesh-Eater, god of Savagery, for he confiscated the property of
> well-born men and distributed it to sycophants and scoundrels . . .[61]

In fact, he was exacting retribution on those who had in any way aided
Brutus, Cassius and the enemy cause, and, as his progress took him ever
further south, it was inevitable that he should be minded to call to account
the queen of Egypt, too. What, after all, had Cleopatra done in the war?
Had the legions she had sent out to fight Crassus really deserted – or was
their decision really Cleopatra's idea all along? What, too, of the fleet she
claimed to have led out to help Octavian and Antony? Had a storm really
driven it back home, or had she, in fact, never really meant to come to
Greece at all? There were clearly questions to be answered and loyalties
to be assessed. So, Antony despatched his trusted lieutenant Dellius to
Alexandria with a summons. The queen of Egypt was to come to Tarsus
for an interview.

Cleopatra's first reactions to this peremptory request are not recorded.
Her subsequent response has entered history. Using all that she knew
of Antony – the consummate performer, the unrivalled impresario, the
playboy, the wit, the great seducer – she galvanized all Alexandria into
frenzied but hard-focused action. This, after all, was an encounter which
would require not only her own peerless wisdom and charisma but the
combined expertise of the royal household and the ingenuity of the
museum staff. For it was critical that this first meeting between queen
and newly powerful general should make its mark.

So, some time in the summer of 41 BC, to the sweep and creek of many
oars, Queen Cleopatra journeyed north from Alexandria, leaving the turbid
waters of the Delta mouth, the sand-suffused warm breeze behind her,
her course set for the lush well-watered meadows which fringed the rich
metropolis of Tarsus, and her first crucial interview with Antony.

Dionysus with wine cup
and thyrsus leans on
a lyre-playing Silenus.
Wall-painting from a
villa at Boscoreale, near
Pompeii, c.30 BC. Height
76 cm. British Museum,
1899,0215.1.

CHAPTER 6

Love Affair

TARSUS: SUMMER 41 BC

ANTONY WAS IN THE MARKET PLACE when the news first reached him. He was seated on the tribunal, the raised platform, the al fresco public office at the heart of Tarsus, conducting the affairs of state. Tarsus was a bustling provincial capital, first city of Cilicia, a rich and fertile land whose patchwork plains were golden with their millet fields, yellow with their flowers of sesame, or silver-grey with olive trees shimmering in serried ranks, their dark trunks casting twisted shadows in the morning sun, while already to the east the densely wooded mountains were dissolving in the haze. Here in Tarsus, Antony had every reason to feel in complete control. Not only was he himself one of the empire's three most powerful men; Cilicia, Tarsus, even the market place in which he sat had been added to that empire sixty years before (103 BC) by Antony's own grandfather.

Yet, this morning he became aware of a strange excitement in the crowds which milled at his feet below the tribunal, of a commotion, a hubbub, a rapid rumour, as people began to leave the market place, first in small groups, then in a greater surge. As Antony was left bewildered on his fast-deserted tribunal, he at last found out the cause. 'Aphrodite' he was told 'had come to revel with Dionysus for the good of Asia'.[62]

Plutarch, who reports all this, does not record what Antony did next. It is unlikely, though, that Antony resisted joining the great throng and seeing for himself the cause of their excitement. For, on the river Cydnus (its broad and reedy banks the haunt of Purple Swamphens, Graceful Warblers, White-throated Kingfishers, its limpid waters broken now by dripping oars) was being staged one of the most dramatic entrances the ancient world had ever seen. The Queen of Egypt, Cleopatra, had arrived in style.

She sailed up the River Cydnus in a barge with a gilded stern, and its purple sails billowed in the breeze as its oarsmen worked their silver oars, in time to the melodies of flutes, accompanied by syrinxes and lyres. The queen herself reclined beneath an awning worked with gold, adorned like Aphrodite in a painting, while on the other side (again like in a painting) stood boys dressed up as Cupids, fanning

Half-god, half-snake, Dionysus and Isis, wearing Egyptian crowns, intertwine their tails. Sandstone stele, from Egypt, 1st century BC. Height 41 cm. British Museum, 1911,0617.22.

The Disembarkation of Cleopatra at Tarsus by Claude Lorrain (1600–82). 1643–82. Pen and brown ink on paper, 199 x 263 cm. British Museum, 1957,1214.69.

her. Likewise, the fairest of her handmaids, costumed, some as Nereids, and some as Graces, took the rudders or the mooring-ropes, and gorgeous perfumes, rising up from countless censers, drifted out across the river banks.[63]

In concept and in execution, this coming of the queen to meet the Roman general had been pitched perfectly. A mere six years before, Cleopatra, twenty-one years old, had sailed with Caesar up the Nile to reveal to him the wondrous fecundity of Egypt. Now, 'at that age when women are most beautiful and their minds are most acute', as Plutarch somewhat chauvinistically expressed it,[64] she had taken to the water once again. But this time, the prize she was exhibiting was not her country; this time, it was herself.

Everything about her coming was calculated to ensnare Mark Antony, from the exuberance of the spectacle to the promises implied by Cleopatra's costume. For here was the Egyptian Isis dressed as Aphrodite, her Greek counterpart; here was a goddess made flesh and come to claim as her godly consort the man who styled himself the human incarnation of divine Dionysus; here was the queen of the richest country of the East symbolically offering the fruits of union to the greatest general of Rome.

That Cleopatra had been summoned to Tarsus to account for her conduct in the Roman civil wars must (with Antony's first glimpse of her) already have seemed quite irrelevant for, even before she disembarked, it was clear that, in a monumental gamble worthy of her mentor Caesar himself, the queen intended to attempt to lay down the rules by which this latest and most crucial game would be played out.

From the start, she gained the initiative. A dinner invitation arrived from Antony. Cleopatra rejected it. As queen of Egypt she ranked higher than a Roman triumvir, and etiquette demanded that Cleopatra host this meal. Antony acquiesced, and by doing so played directly into Cleopatra's hand. For this was to be no ordinary dinner. It was to be a tour de force. When Antony arrived

> he found that the arrangements defied description, but what amazed him most was the sheer number of lights. It is said that so many of these were suspended from the roof and arranged on every side and all at once, set out and grouped in such ingenious patterns, some in rectangles, some in circles, that few spectacles have been so brilliant and beautiful.

If the flickering lights were magical, the fabrics, plates and goblets which their brilliance illuminated were opulent beyond imagination.

> All were made of solid gold; the bowls were exquisitely crafted and studded with jewels; and the walls, they say, were hung with tapestries interwoven with gold threads.[65]

Like a moth drawn to the flame, Antony was spellbound. When Cleopatra 'quietly smiled' and told him that everything he saw was (in true Alexandrian tradition) a present 'just for him', he was truly captivated. As the evening ended, she invited Antony back for more. The next night

> she hosted a reception so much more splendid than the first that the decorations made the previous one seem mean; again she presented them to Antony. Moreover, she let each of his staff-officers keep the couch on which he had reclined – and the tables, too, as well as the fabrics on the couches, were divided up among them. When they left, she provided litters (with bearers) for those of higher rank, while

to the majority she supplied horses adorned with silvered harnesses. With all of them she dispatched Ethiopian slave-boys as lamp-bearers. On the fourth day she bought a talent's worth of roses, and caused the dining room floors to be spread with them a cubit deep [about 40 cm/16 in].

When Antony tried to reciprocate, inviting Cleopatra and her court to dine with him, it was an abject failure. Fortunately, however, Antony was not a man to take himself too seriously, but even his attempts to gloss over his shortcomings were closely studied by the queen, for she had made it her mission to discover all there was to know about the general and mould her own behaviour that it might best suit his. As Plutarch put it:

> Antony issued his own invitation to dinner in return. He was keen to outdo her in brilliance and elegance, but in neither was he successful; and he was the first to mock the squalor and rusticity of his arrangements. Cleopatra observed that Antony's humour was earthy, that of a soldier or a workman, so, confidently and without holding back, she adopted the same manner towards him.[66]

At some point in these heady days, Antony must have remembered why he had summoned Cleopatra. The historian Appian (no admirer of either party) suggests that, while Antony 'took her to task for taking no part in the campaign to avenge Caesar', Cleopatra 'did not excuse herself' but claimed (quite truthfully) that, while she had tried to do so, events had intervened (see pp. 84–5).[67] By now, however, it probably made little difference what she said. Already, to use Plutarch's brisk assessment, 'Antony was ravished',[68] or as Appian put it:

> As soon as he saw her, Antony lost his head to her, as if he was a young man, although he was forty years old.[69]

Cleopatra had achieved at least the first of her objectives. Now, with winter approaching, she sought to build on her success. In a move, no doubt already calculated and prepared for, she suggested to Antony that, rather than overwintering in Asia or Greece as he had no doubt intended, he should come to Alexandria instead. It can have come as a surprise to nobody that he agreed.

First, though, Cleopatra had one outstanding piece of family business to attend to. For the past five years, her sister Arsinoë, who had once been paraded through the streets of Rome in Caesar's triumph, had been living in the temple complex at Ephesus, serving as a priestess of the goddess Artemis. Out of sight she may have been, but for Cleopatra's enemies Arsinoë was never far from their minds. Only a year earlier (42 BC), malcontents had begun addressing her as 'queen'. As long as she lived, she would remain a rival for the throne of Egypt. It was clearly time for her to die. So, in one of his first acts of loving kindness to Cleopatra, Antony gave her request his blessing. At Ephesus, a special unit of his men escorted Arsinoë from the temple, sweet with incense, and on the marble steps which led up to its doors (so delicately carved in ivory) they butchered her.

Elsewhere throughout the provinces of Asia there were more deaths. With only one exception (the high priest at Ephesus), any who had shown support or sympathy for Cleopatra's sister were tracked down and killed. So, on the island of Aradus (Arwad) off the coast of Syria, a young man was dragged roughly from an altar. He was, he claimed, the king of Egypt, Ptolemy XIII, Cleopatra's brother, whose army had been beaten six years earlier by Caesar in the Alexandrian War, whose corpse had never been recovered from the Nile (see p. 54). The soldiers sent by Antony to Aradus took great care that this fresh corpse was put on the most public display possible. The message was clear. Cleopatra VII, Queen of Egypt, Father-Loving Goddess, had no surviving siblings.

Luxury, wealth and style: a pair of gold earrings in the form of lynx heads and amphoras. c.100–50 BC. Length 4.8 cm. British Museum, 1872,0604.1105.

Her business successfully concluded, Cleopatra returned to Alexandria. As the autumn squalls gave way to winter, Antony too returned. He knew the city well. It held fond memories. Perhaps (being a romantic) he had already told the queen that he had been

> aroused by her years earlier when, a young cavalry officer on Gabinius' expedition to Alexandria, he had seen her, still a girl.[70]

Indeed, it seemed as if the triumvir were trying to recapture that lost youth, exploring every hedonistic avenue the city had to offer, immersing himself, in the disapproving words of Plutarch the moralist, 'in the recreations and amusements of a carefree youth'.[71] Whereas for Caesar's restless mind Alexandria had been a constant source of inspiration and ideas, for Antony, the pleasure-seeker, the same city offered endless opportunities for decadence; and Cleopatra was more than happy to encourage him.

> Whatever Antony's mood, whether grave or carefree, she could always find a new pleasure to delight him. She was his constant tutor

and never once let him go by night or day. She played dice with him; she drank with him; she hunted with him; she watched him as he exercised with weapons. At night, when he wandered the city, standing by the doors or windows of the poorer peoples' houses and mocking those inside, she accompanied him in his foolish games, dressed in the costume of a maidservant while Antony was disguised as a slave ... The Alexandrians (themselves by no means coarse or uncultivated) loved coarse ways and played along with him.[72]

It was as if they were following the advice carved on the grave-stone of the dead Tayimhotep to her husband Pasherenptah, the high priest who had officiated at the coronation of Cleopatra's father, Ptolemy the Flautist:

Oh my brother, my husband, friend, high Priest! Do not weary of drinking, eating, getting intoxicated and making love! Make holiday! Follow your heart day and night! Let not care into your heart otherwise what use are your years upon earth?

Indeed, using the language of theatre, which always seemed to spring to mind whenever anyone spoke of Antony, the people of Alexandria are reported to have said that he 'put on his tragic mask for the Romans, but kept the comic one for them'.[73]

Everybody had a story about Antony that winter. Most featured the club which (in appropriately adolescent mode) Cleopatra and he set up, and whose name is perhaps best rendered as the *Society of Peerless Bon Viveurs*.[74] Confined to their most intimate circle of wealthy friends, the purpose of this club was for members to host daily banquets on a rotating basis 'of an almost incredible extravagance'.[75] Even Plutarch, generations later, could record an account of one such evening, told first-hand to his grandfather by a friend, a physician, Lamprias, who happened to be studying in Alexandria and managed to have himself smuggled into the royal kitchens where

he saw the lavishness of food and drink and watched eight wild boars being roasted. When he observed that there must surely be a vast number of guests, the cook laughed and said: 'No, there are not many guests, only about twelve; but everything must be cooked and served to perfection. Even a minute's delay might ruin things. Maybe Antony will demand the meal immediately, or in a short while; or maybe he will delay it while he calls for wine or if he's in the middle of a conversation. So, since it is very hard to judge the right timing, we make not one dinner but many.'[76]

The outlay was undoubtedly prodigious if not profligate, and, especially given the run of bad harvests that had plagued Egypt in recent years, it could not be allowed to go on for ever. Besides, whether in the telling or in fact, Antony's behaviour seemed, if anything, to have become progressively more excessive as the winter dragged on. Less than a century later, anecdotes were still told of how he started to 'use golden vessels when satisfying the basest needs of nature, disgraceful behaviour that would have brought shame on Cleopatra'.[77]

As for Cleopatra herself, she may have been an amiable and spirited companion, ready to match Antony step for step on his path to ever greater self-indulgence, but she remained a powerful single-minded queen, capable of getting her own way; and in the end it seems to have been Cleopatra who decided to call time on Antony's stay in Alexandria. The manner in

A short distance from the temple where Arsinoë was murdered, the Arcadian Way leads from the theatre at Ephesus to the (now silted) harbour.

95

which she did this reveals much about her personality. The source is once more Plutarch, who may have been drawing on further stories told at first hand to his grandfather:

> Antony was fishing one day, but he caught nothing, which irritated him, especially since Cleopatra was present. So he gave orders to his fishermen to dive down and secretly to fasten onto his hook some fish, which he had caught previously. In this way, he pulled in his line two or three times. But Cleopatra was not fooled. She pretended to be amazed, told her friends and invited them to come the next day to observe Antony's skill. Huge numbers of them clambered into fishing boats, and when Antony had let down his line, she ordered one of her servants to swim at once down to his hook and fasten on a salted fish from the Black Sea. Antony thought that he had caught something and reeled it in to much mirth, as one might expect. 'My general', said Cleopatra, 'let us poor rulers of Pharos and Canopus keep our fishing rods. Cities, kingdoms, continents should be your prey.'[78]

The face of Fulvia? The bust of winged Victory is thought to bear the features of Antony's wife. Gold *aureus*, struck at Rome, 41 BC. British Museum, R.9272.

The message (though sugared) was clear. Antony had business to attend to elsewhere. Admittedly, at least inasmuch as the winter weather had allowed, he had been keeping himself as much abreast as possible with news from Italy. Indeed, as he read reports from Rome, he might have felt it was both timely and convenient for him to be so far away. For, while he and Cleopatra had been taking their ease in Alexandria, not only Antony's wife, Fulvia, but also his brother Lucius, had been making their presence felt in the empire's capital.

Both were strong individuals; but although Lucius enjoyed political authority – he had been one of the two consuls for 41 BC – it was Fulvia who wielded the greater power. Antony was her third husband. Her first had been Caesar's controversial fixer, the wealthy, aristocratic but utterly cold-hearted Clodius, whose gangs of thugs once terrorized the streets of Rome as they sought to impose their masters' will by any means. Her second husband, Scribonius Curio, moneyed, well-connected, one of Caesar's chief lieutenants, had died fighting in North Africa (49 BC); and it had been Fulvia's marriage two years later to Mark Antony that, as much as anything, had helped him not only pay his increasingly mounting debts but regain Caesar's favour and return to power (see p. 79). Now Caesar had been murdered, Fulvia was playing her own important role in Roman politics. For not only was she Antony's wife; her daughter Clodia was married to Octavian. More even than their colleague Lepidus, Fulvia was at the heart of the triumvirate.

Had it not been for Fulvia's being born a woman in a world where only men could enter politics, she would herself have been a major player in the public life of Rome. She certainly possessed all the credentials. There was about her, as one commentator born a generation later, wrote, 'nothing of the woman except her sex'. It had been she (so it was claimed) who had taken such delight in piercing with her hairpins the tongue of the dead Cicero, and Plutarch (while noting in passing that, even with Fulvia, Antony had attempted to lighten their relationship through practical jokes) commented:

> This was a woman with no care for spinning or for housekeeping, a woman not content to preside over a husband who remained a private citizen; rather her ambition was to rule a ruler and command a commander. So Cleopatra was in Fulvia's debt for schooling Antony to be submissive to a woman, since, when she took him over, he was already broken in and trained to obey a woman's wishes.[79]

But even Fulvia could not keep her place for long. As a wife, she could (with patience) be endured; as a mother-in-law she soon became intolerable. Even for the sake of politics, Octavian could put up with her no longer.

> Preferring to seem to be in disagreement with Fulvia rather than with Antony, he divorced her daughter [Clodia], claiming on oath that she was still a virgin. He showed little concern that anyone should speculate as to why the girl was still a virgin after having lived with him for so long – whether it might suggest that he had already planned in advance to divorce her, or whether it might be for another reason.[80]

Now, furious for her daughter's sake and with her husband far away in Egypt, Fulvia allied herself with Lucius, Antony's younger brother. Perhaps, as was suggested, she was motivated, too, by 'a woman's jealousy' that Antony was overwintering with Cleopatra; more likely she was following a shrewd political agenda of her own. Their manifesto was to ease the plight of the farmers of Italy, who had been evicted from their fields to provide land on which the veterans of the civil war might settle; the focus of their anger was Octavian.

They swiftly raised an army from among the dispossessed and, for a short time, occupied the two towns of Perusia (Perugia) and Praeneste (Palestrina). But with almost equal speed Octavian responded. Soon the rebels were under siege, and, as the chefs of Alexandria cooked their uneaten meals for Antony, the people of Perusia were starved into submission. By the time of Antony's fishing trips with Cleopatra, Lucius, whom one historian dismissed as 'sharing the faults of his brother but possessing none of the virtues which he occasionally showed', had surrendered. So, too, had Fulvia.

Their dangerous attempt at opposition to Octavian had failed. Yet, for the Roman world it could have been much more disastrous. The so-called Perusine War could easily have sparked another civil war. Octavian, however, calculating, canny, and with his eye already on the longer game, chose to spare both Fulvia, who fled to Greece, and Lucius, whom he sent to Spain as governor. The people of Perusia were not so fortunate.

As for Antony, he could legitimately claim ignorance of the whole affair. What influence, after all, could he have wielded from so far away as Egypt? Besides, he was quite occupied enough with other things. What is so remarkable is that people seemed to be quite ready to accept his version of events. Dio, for one, appears to give it total credence. Writing of Antony's first years as triumvir, he observes:

> He was so led by passion and drunkenness that he gave no thought either to his allies or to his enemies. True, while he was of junior rank, still striving for the first prize, he had devoted himself seriously to his duties; but now he had attained power, he no longer cared anything for any of these things. Instead, he joined Cleopatra and the Egyptians in their life of luxurious leisure, until he became completely sapped.[81]

How convenient for Antony to have such a convincing excuse.

All in all, then, his winter stay in Alexandria had served its purpose very satisfactorily indeed – for both general and queen. As she watched Antony's war galley sail away, its oar-blades churning the deep waters of the royal harbour, and then, past Pharos island, its purple sail unfurling, Cleopatra could permit herself one of her 'quiet smiles'. When she had met the Roman, she was still under suspicion for collaborating with his enemies. Now she could rely on his alliance and support – just as she had relied on Caesar's. Moreover, there was one more similarity with her relationship with Caesar, another cause for her complacency, of which even Antony as he sailed might not have been aware. It may have still been relatively early days, but Cleopatra was pregnant.

Undoubtedly the queen had taken stock of Antony; of equal certainty must be that she had quickly realized he was no Caesar. Yet he was still one of the three most powerful men in Rome, and patronage in Rome was what Cleopatra and her country, Egypt, needed most. Political necessity had demanded that she form a strong alliance with a powerful Roman, while circumstance had dictated that he should be Antony. His, after all, was the jurisdiction over all the East; and he was so susceptible.

Besides, there was much in Antony which must have been attractive: his military prowess and charisma, so like Caesar's; his passion for the arts and the dramatic, so like the passion of Cleopatra's own late father, Ptolemy the Flautist; and, unlike either man, he was so much more close to Cleopatra's age; he was so much more malleable.

Now that she was carrying his child, it did not matter that Antony was gone from Alexandria. In fact, it was essential that he was. His place was not in Egypt but in the wider Roman world. For him to hold and build his powerbase, as Cleopatra needed him to do if he were still to help her, Antony must keep on doing what he so far had done so well: campaign for Rome and play the game of politics against Octavian. As his ship disappeared in the haze of the horizon, Cleopatra may well have thought that Antony, like Caesar, had departed, never to return. Yet in his hands now lay the fate of Egypt.

Antony's views are perhaps more difficult to imagine, though subsequent events might suggest that Cleopatra had made more of an impact upon Antony than he had upon Cleopatra. Now, though, he ordered his helmsman to steer a course northwards, first to Syria and thence to Athens. Here, more surely than at Alexandria, he was forced to turn his wandering attention back towards affairs of empire and his awkward alliance with Octavian.

Reminders of just how awkward this alliance truly was were everywhere, not least in Antony's own apartments. Fulvia, his wife, fresh from the debacle of the Perusine War, had come to Athens too and so, independently, had his mother Julia. Both women had their tale to tell and, for Antony, neither was entirely pleasing. Fulvia's failed rebellion in Italy was bad enough, but at least it had not led to disastrous consequences. His mother Julia, on the other hand, had come fresh from fraternizing with a man who arguably had gained the status of 'Rome's most wanted': Sextus Pompey, son of Caesar's ancient enemy, had seized control of grain-rich Sicily and was assembling an army. Now, through Julia, he offered to throw in his hand with Antony into a war against Octavian.

Nor was he alone. Survivors of the Perusine War were sending messages to Antony pledging their support, outlining their strategies, assuring him that they had 'prepared disembarkation points and supplies for him at various locations in Italy, anticipating that he would come at once'. For as long as he could, Antony refused to rise to their challenge. Instead, he prevaricated, preferring to spend his time cementing his image as the new Dionysus, the peace-bringing saviour of Rome's eastern empire. A near contemporary described how

> later, while Antony himself was spending time in Athens, he caused a gazebo to be built above the theatre, closely thatched with green wood to resemble a grotto sacred to Dionysus; in it he hung drums and fawn-skins and all the other Dionysiac paraphernalia, and from early morning onwards he would recline there getting drunk with his friends – while a group of hired musicians brought over from Italy played constantly, and all the Greeks gathered for the spectacle. At times he strolled up to the Acropolis, and lamps were hung from the roofs, illuminating the whole city of Athens; and from that time on he ordered that he should be proclaimed throughout every city as Dionysus.[82]

What Cleopatra thought, if she ever learned of this, we do not know. On the one hand, the detail of the lamps would have amused her – how well already Antony had learned from her example! On the other hand, she cannot but have felt a growing uneasiness at Antony's behaviour. If, as appeared likely, war was brewing, he seemed very unprepared.

At last he made a move. Leaving Fulvia in Greece, he crossed the Ionian Sea to anchor in Italy at Brundisium (Brindisi). But the port authorities denied him access. Antony mounted a blockade. Conflict seemed inevitable. With an Italian city over which he had direct command now under siege, Octavian too rallied troops and marched east to Brundisium. The two men's armies faced each other. Tensions mounted. Cavalrymen clashed. But the mood among the rank and file was not for fighting, and when they heard that Fulvia, the wife of one, the other's erstwhile mother-in-law, had fallen ill and died, Octavian and Antony used the news as a pretext to make peace.

After all, it had been Fulvia, not Antony, who had conducted the Perusine War. Now that she was dead, let Fulvia take all the blame for everything and let her death diffuse such tensions as remained. For both men, it was such a convenient untruth. Antony's consort would become a scapegoat. The focus of Octavian's ire would be not Antony but the woman who had abused her privileged position at his side. It was a fine solution – and a precedent.

In their glow of reconciliation, Octavian and Antony hosted banquets in each others' honour, 'Octavian in military and Roman fashion and Antony in Asiatic and Egyptian style'.[83] No doubt there were more hanging lights. A treaty was signed (September 40 BC) which granted all the western provinces to Octavian and all the eastern to Antony. To Antony, too, went, as token of his great esteem and trust, his colleague's sister, Octavia, coincidentally the same age as Cleopatra and, like her, forceful, educated and intelligent. To Lepidus, their fellow triumvir, went Africa, and peace (of a sort) was made with Sextus Pompey.

At some point during these oddly heady days, perhaps in the first flush of marriage, Antony and Octavia must have received a no doubt exuberant announcement, transmitted with pomp and ceremony through the usual diplomatic channels from Egypt. In Alexandria, Cleopatra's pregnancy had come to term and she had given birth: to twins, a boy and girl, Antony's children. They were half-siblings to Caesar's son Caesarion, and heirs to the ancient throne of Egypt.

How the newly-weds received the news we can but speculate. The marriage of Antony and Octavia was based not on love but on politics, but because it was so politically vital, because on its precarious success hung the future of that other union between the two triumvirs, Octavian and Antony, it was all the more important that its harmony should not be jeopardized. What would jeopardize it most, of course, was any sign of an ongoing dalliance between Antony and Cleopatra. In marrying his colleague to his sister, Octavian had (with characteristic efficiency and keen-eyed calculation) sought to ensure that, for Antony, any future relationship with fecund Egypt must be purely diplomatic.

Wedded harmony: Antony and Octavia grace the obverse of a silver *cistophorus* coin while Dionysus dominates the reverse. The coin was struck in Asia Minor, c.39 BC. Diam. 2.6 cm. British Museum, G.2205.

For Cleopatra, this was an admirable outcome. It let her govern Egypt without interference, safe in the knowledge that, as long as the Roman Empire was secure and its foreign policy remained the same, there would be every likelihood that her own position would be unassailable. In the long months which followed, she could bask in the glow of her success, reflecting, perhaps, that as her teacher Caesar boasted he had done in Pontus, in Tarsus she, too, had 'come, seen and conquered', winning an all-too-easy victory hands-down.

Yet, Cleopatra still left nothing to chance. Embedded in Antony's household was an intelligence agent, an Egyptian soothsayer, charged with promoting the queen's interests and ensuring that reliable reports came back to Alexandria. Given this agent's cover, it was inevitable that some of these reports were less worldly than others. Thus Cleopatra might learn that the soothsayer had

> advised Antony to keep as far away as he could from the young Octavian, saying 'Your daimon [guardian spirit] is afraid of his: it may be confident and proud when it is on its own, but it becomes base and craven when his is nearby.' Indeed, events appeared to bear out the Egyptian's words, for it is said that whenever the two men (for whatever reason) played games together – casting lots or rolling dice – Antony invariably lost . . . Antony tried to hide his annoyance when this happened, but it caused him to listen more closely to the Egyptian's warnings. So he entrusted Octavian with the running of his household and left Italy.[84]

Not for the last time, the dodgy conclusions of the intelligence community had led to political outcomes; but on this occasion they were benign. By the end of the next year, Cleopatra would have heard how Antony, with his wife Octavia and new-born daughter Antonia firmly at his side, had returned to Athens where he would spend the winter (39–38 BC).

It may not have been quite such a self-indulgent spree as his stay in Alexandria had been two years before, but this season in the Greek capital was, in its own way, memorable. Basking in what he perceived as his renewed and reinvigorated alliance with Octavian, Antony felt he could relax. With his young wife charming the Athenians,

> he kept an eye on military reports, but that was all. Once more he exchanged the role of commander for that of private citizen, wearing simple Greek clothing with Athenian sandals, and enjoying a quiet lifestyle . . . He took his meals in the Greek manner, exercised with the Greeks, and enjoyed their festivals in Octavia's company. For (being a man who easily fell in love with women) he was infatuated by her.[85]

Although Plutarch lays more stress on Antony's official roles, he paints a similar picture:

> Antony . . . took on the role of gymnasiarch for the Athenians. He left at home his insignia of command, and appeared in public carrying the gymnasiarch's rods and wearing Greek robes and white shoes.[86]

Yet, in the midst of such admirably civic pursuits, Antony still found time to pursue two of his intensely personal interests: bolstering his reputation as a god throughout the East and ensuring that his coffers continued to be filled,

> calling himself the youthful Dionysus and requiring others to address him in this way; and, in the light of both this and of his general behaviour, when the Athenians betrothed Athena to him [an allegorical act, combining religious ritual with political expediency], he said that he accepted the [purely symbolic] marriage but extracted from them a [completely tangible] dowry of four million sesterces.[87]

All in all, however, his winter stay at Athens was a much more staid affair than Alexandria had been. There is no mention anywhere of any 'disgraceful behaviour'.

If there was little in Antony's behaviour in the heart of Greece to cause concern, when the sea-lanes reopened in the spring of 38 BC, news of a very different kind would have begun to filter back to Alexandria.

From Sicily, Cleopatra would have heard how Sextus Pompey was renewing his hostilities with Rome; from Athens, how Antony had once more donned his military uniform to fight against not only Pompey but the Parthians; from Rome itself how fleets were being launched to sail out against Pompey's ships and break the stranglehold he held upon the city's crucial food supply once and for all. Later that year, Cleopatra would have heard of desperate sea-battles, of Pompey's victories, of galleys lost in storms, of Octavian himself (albeit briefly) fleeing for his life. She would have learned, too, how Octavian had called an urgent meeting at Brundisium, of Antony answering his call, of Octavian himself never materializing, leaving Antony, snubbed, to make his way back east to Greece. Yet despite the turmoil in the Roman Empire, Egypt remained untouched. It must have seemed as if the country and its queen were charmed.

As the months wore on (38–37 BC) and the web of reports reaching the Egyptian capital became ever more complex, certain clear headlines nonetheless stood out: a partial victory by one of Antony's lieutenants over Parthia; the future of Antony's alliance with Octavian cemented by the betrothal of their still infant children; Antony agreeing to lend Octavian more than a hundred ships to help him in his ongoing war with Sextus Pompey. Then, from Parthia, news began to filter through that civil war had broken out. From Greece came the intelligence that Antony, quick to exploit this disarray among Rome's ancient enemies, was meaning to amass an expedition. Antioch would be the site of the great levee. True, the situation was fluid and events were moving rapidly, but there was nothing here to menace Egypt.

Then, in the autumn of 37 BC there came to Alexandria another message, which, no matter how prepared it might have been by past intelligence reports, the royal court cannot but have greeted with dismay. At a stroke, the note threatened to endanger the delicately balanced diplomatic equilibrium Cleopatra had for so long worked so cleverly to build. For, contained within the message was a summons. How to respond to it must have taxed even the most gifted brains in Alexandria. Even Cleopatra's. To accept or refuse could cause such great resentment in one camp or the other that it might suddenly and unexpectedly plunge Egypt into war.

As, in the royal palace, Cleopatra stood dismayed, weighing up the implications of the letter, she may have glanced at one of the black basalt sculptures of a sphinx which decorated its wide courtyards; she may have felt that this conundrum facing her was as impossible as any which that creature might have posed.

For the message was from Antony, and it was blunt. He had sent his wife Octavia, his colleague's sister, guarantor of the stability of the triumvirate, back home to Italy. It was with Cleopatra that he wished to spend the coming months in Antioch.

Enigmatic and lethal: a
yellow limestone Sphinx
of the Graeco-Roman
period (1st century BC–
2nd century AD), from
Egypt. Length 41.5 cm;
height 25 cm. British
Museum, 1875,0810.10.

CHAPTER 7

Dark Victory

ANTIOCH: AUTUMN 37 BC

PERHAPS IT WAS the choice of venue that gave Cleopatra the idea. For, just as Alexandria had been the seat of the great Ptolemaic Empire, so Antioch was founded by another of Alexander the Great's generals, Seleucus, as his capital from which to govern Syria.

Like Alexandria, too, Antioch was known for its magnificence, with its broad streets laid out on a grid, its lush, well-watered gardens, its gleaming temples, its theatre and its royal palace. Yet, there were differences as well. In Antioch, the palace was built on an island in the gushing rapid waters of the River Orontes, while to the south the walls of a high citadel climbed up the rock-face of Mount Silpius. With its multi-ethnic population, Greeks and Jews and Syrians, the city could boast perhaps some half a million inhabitants. Only Rome and Alexandria itself housed more.

Now, with the plain stretching on either side of the Orontes transformed into a sea of tents and temporary billets for the prodigious army that Antony intended to lead next year to Parthia, the city's population would soon be swollen by many thousand men, their slaves and their suppliers. The palace, meanwhile, found itself accommodating the royal court of Egypt.

Despite any initial misgivings, Cleopatra had concluded that she must give in to Antony's request, and join him. *He*, after all, had summoned *her*; he needed the support of Egypt for his forthcoming campaign, and surely he would not have invited her if he believed that doing so would antagonize Octavian. Such, at least, may have been the official arguments. Privately, however, based both on her own judgement and on reports from her embedded agent, the Egyptian soothsayer, Cleopatra may well have realized what Plutarch subsequently would spell out:

> That great catastrophe which for so long had lain dormant, namely Antony's passion for Cleopatra, a passion which seemed to have been charmed away or lulled to rest by higher considerations, [had] again

Heroic Antony on a red jasper intaglio for a ring. Roman, c.40–30 BC. Length 1.4 cm. British Museum, 1867,0507.724.

caught light and blazed up once more as he approached the coast of Syria.[88]

If this were the case, Cleopatra would make sure that she (and Egypt) benefited – especially if (as she must have feared) Octavian proved less than enthusiastic about her renewed fraternization with his sister's husband, Antony. If she was to take the risk that travelling to Antioch implied, she must also reap not inconsiderable rewards. The time had clearly come to discuss terms.

Writing in the centuries that followed, historians tended to agree that Antony himself had 'showered her with gifts'. It is more likely that Cleopatra arrived with a wish-list. Certainly, within a short time of her arrival, the Egyptian queen found that her empire had become significantly enlarged:

> In addition to the territories which she already held, Antony presented her with Phoenicia, Coele Syria, Cyprus and a large area of Cilicia; and, in addition, the part of Judaea which produces balsam and the coastal strip of Arabia Nabataea stretching down to the Red Sea.[89]

In fact, with the addition of these territories, almost the entire area of the Ptolemaic Empire as it had once existed in its heyday (third century BC) had been restored to Cleopatra. Only the heartland of Judaea and kingdom of Nabataea were denied her. With complete justification, Cleopatra could now issue an edict back in Egypt proclaiming that this year (37–36 BC) should henceforth be known not only as the 'Year Sixteen' of her reign, but as 'Year One'. In official records throughout her territories it was thus recorded that, on 1 September 37 BC, had begun the Second Empire of the Ptolemies.

Nor was this all. Again, prompted by Cleopatra, Antony publicly acknowledged his paternity of her twins, now three years old. In a naming ceremony, possibly (given his predilection for display) held in the great theatre at Antioch, Antony presented to the people his two children, to be known henceforth as Alexander Helios (the Sun) and Cleopatra Selene (the Moon). The symbolism could not have been more palpable. Not only did the names unite the first Ptolemaic Empire with the second, linking the name of the present queen with that of the great founder of Alexandria himself; with their addition of the epithets 'Helios' and 'Selene', they solemnly identified the royal children as the human incarnations of two of the great gods of the empire's east. Like both their parents, they were to be regarded as divine.

In Rome, reaction to Antony's decisions was at best lukewarm. 'The gift of the territories especially irritated the Romans', while his acknowledgement of the two children simply 'made the scandal worse'.[90] At least Octavian could not, in any seriousness, have complained about identifying the twins with gods. The truth was that in Rome Octavian himself had been doing his best to carve out a connection with the divine Apollo, hosting a banquet at which (with quite uncharacteristic flamboyance) he had appeared dressed as the god:

> At this [banquet] the guests took their places at table dressed as gods and goddesses, while Octavian himself was costumed as Apollo. This charge was laid against him not only in correspondence of Antony, who bitterly lists all present, but also in the well-known, if anonymous, poem: ". . . while [Octavian] Caesar sacrilegiously and hypocritically took the role of Apollo, and conducts his unconventionally debauched banquet of the gods, all the true deities turned their backs on the earth and Jupiter himself fled from his golden throne."[91]

The imperial biographer Suetonius goes on to comment that, given the fact that Sextus Pompey was again interfering with Rome's food supplies, the timing of the banquet was less than sensitive.

> What increased the scandal of this banquet was the poverty and famine which gripped Italy at the time. The next day there were public complaints that the gods had eaten all the grain and, while Octavian was indeed Apollo, he

The divine conception of Octavian? The Portland Vase may show Apollo's sea-snake impregnating Octavian's mother, Atia. Cameo glass from Rome, c. AD 1–25. Height 24.5 cm. British Museum, 1945,0927.1, purchased with the aid of a bequest from James Rose Vallentin.

was Apollo the Executioner. This is a title by which the god used to be worshipped in one district of Rome.[92]

In fact, by setting himself up as Apollo, a god with whom he would identify himself for the rest of his long life, Octavian was quite consciously positioning himself as the antithesis of Antony. Dionysus, the god in whose guise Antony was fêted in the east of the empire, was a god of exuberant emotion, of abandon, merriment and excess. Apollo on the other hand was altogether more austere, a god of reason and of rigour, a god of harmony and of the type of order which is achieved by following the rules.

In the East, too, Apollo had his devotees. Just outside Antioch, in the leafy suburbs of Daphne, with its laurels and its oak groves and its waterfalls, was a famous precinct of the god, with a fabulously wealthy temple and a great cult statue carved by the master Bryaxis, whose work adorned the Mausoleum in Halicarnassus far to the north-west, yet another of the wonders of the ancient world. Yet, despite the presence of the stern Apollo's temple, Daphne was to Antioch what Canopus was to Alexandria: a place of pleasure and lax morals. As such it surely held no small attraction for Antony. That no accounts have survived of partying and excess during these winter months does not mean that there was none. Certainly Antony and Cleopatra renewed the physical relationship they had enjoyed at Alexandria, for by the end of winter the queen was once more pregnant.

But in late spring, even the relaxed tranquillity of Daphne would be shattered (May 36 BC). It must have seemed as if all Antioch was on the move. As the tents were struck and the billets taken down, the city must have echoed to the clash of marching boots on marble flagstones, the thud of hooves, the rumble of the wheels of mobile missile launchers. For it was time to march on Parthia, and Antony could wait no longer. With assurances from Cleopatra that she would do all that she could to augment his navy and to keep his troops supplied, he set the queen on her journey back to Egypt and gave his men the order to advance.

As the dust began to settle and the army disappeared from view, Cleopatra could at last take stock. For much had changed. Her empire had expanded overnight, but it was not only new territories that she now controlled, but new business ventures, too, with attractive possibilities for newly increased revenues. Like a powerful chief executive after a successful merger, Cleopatra now found herself at the head of a multinational organization, requiring careful administration and strong leadership.

Among the ventures she had newly inherited, Cleopatra now controlled the lucrative trade routes between the Mediterranean in the west and both India and Sri Lanka in the east, with all the possibilities this brought not only for taxation but also for building diplomatic ties. Closer to home, she now held the franchise on the profitable balsam industry, supplying aromatic resin used in the manufacture of both fragrances and ointments. So valuable was this trade that she brought balsam cuttings from Jericho, which until now had controlled the business, to Egypt, where the shrubs were now grown on an industrial scale.

Two other businesses had more immediate benefits, not just for Cleopatra but for Antony too. The hills of Cleopatra's newly annexed provinces of Cyprus and Cilicia, Lebanon and Gilead were thickly forested, their cedars, pines and oaks the raw materials for oars and galleys needed to equip Antony's new navy, which would require not only warships, but vital transport vessels too. To seal the hulls of these new ships required a thick black coat of bitumen, and over this concession, too, Cleopatra ruled supreme. The only other elements needed for shipbuilding were the linen sails, the twisted ropes, the expertise and manpower – and Egypt possessed all these already in abundance. Caesar had seen how quickly Alexandrians could build and man a fleet to fight against him (see p. 50); now Cleopatra would supply a fleet for Antony.

Of course, not everyone was happy for their territory or business to be taken over. In Judaea, the troublesome king Herod tried to swallow his resentment and offered to collect the revenue for Cleopatra on her Dead Sea bitumen franchise. Cleopatra accepted his suggestion, but with reservations. In the throes of domestic troubles of his own, the Roman client king resented Cleopatra, not only for her greater power but for what he perceived as her interference in purely Jewish affairs. An Egyptian fluent in both Hebrew and Aramaic, she had challenged his choice of candidate to be High Priest, and, with the backing of Antony, had ensured the appointment of her own nominee. Herod was incandescent, but there was nothing he could do, except announce a few months later that the new High Priest had accidentally drowned. Herod took childish glee not only in his utterly unlikely boasts that Cleopatra had once attempted to seduce him, but in his so much more believable claims that he had considered having the queen killed. He was not a pleasant man.

At Rome, too, eyebrows were being raised. All the territories now in Cleopatra's hands had, after all, been under the direct command of Rome. Although it might have made strategic sense for Antony to have transferred their governance to someone he could trust to rule them with integrity, this did not minimize the fact that he had, in effect, relinquished a significant part of the Roman Empire to an independent foreign queen. For patriotic Romans this was unacceptable.

In the East, however, Cleopatra's star burned ever brighter. At Antioch new coins were struck. On one side they showed Antony; on the other Cleopatra, in the guise not of the goddess Isis now but of a Roman matriarch. Meanwhile she not only assigned to herself new titles, 'Lover of her Fatherland', 'The Younger Goddess', but she used the imagery now associated with her children to bolster the perception of her own divinity. For with their new names Helios and Selene, Sun and Moon, her young twins played an increasingly important role in Cleopatra's propaganda.

Throughout the Greek world, the sun and moon were themselves viewed as twins, associates of Victory, while for centuries in Egypt the moon had been identified with Isis, the goddess in whose incarnation Cleopatra was increasingly being worshipped. In Egypt, too, for 1,500 years the pharaohs had been worshipped as the embodiment of the sun, not least in the great temple complex at the City of the Sun, Heliopolis, while in the scholarly studies of Alexandria, Greek poets had written hymns in deliberately archaizing language describing how

> Helios, like unto th' immortal gods,
> shines his light on mortal men and th' immortal gods
> as he urges on his chariot team of horses. His eyes flash fiercely
> from beneath his golden helmet; dazzling rays
> flare bright from him and the gleaming hair
> cascading from his temples frames so gracefully
> his far-beaming face. A rich, fine-woven
> garment shimmers on his body and quivers as the
> breezes blow . . .[93]

In the wider East, too, and throughout the Mediterranean, the sun was worshipped as the harbinger of a new epoch of peace and harmony, the Golden Age which, after decades of destructive civil war, so many yearned for.

Yet Egypt and the Graeco-Roman world were not alone in worshipping the sun. In Parthia, the new king Phraates IV proclaimed that he was 'Brother of the Sun and Moon', but fraternal love for Antony's young children was not part of his agenda. For by summer 36 BC, Antony, back in his role as Roman general, was already riding at the head of his vast, lumbering army, its men, pack animals and wagons snaking back for miles behind him, their mission: once and for all to smash the Parthians.

The sun-god wears a radiate crown on a silver *denarius* of Antony. Struck at a travelling mint in 42 BC. Diam. 1.85 cm. British Museum, 1868,0514.61.

Antony had already made his preparations well. Rather than attempt to launch a direct attack east into Parthia as might have been expected, he had chosen instead to march first north-east to Armenia, where the apparently reliable king, Ardavastes, had pledged his full support. From here he would swoop south to Parthia. So, in Armenia, at a place already pre-arranged, he met his allies. Plutarch describes the vast resources now at Antony's command:

> There were sixty thousand actual Romans, together with cavalry classed as the Romans, made up of ten thousand Iberians and Celts. There were thirty thousand men of other nationalities, including cavalry and light-armed troops.[94]

Even if the total figure of 100,000 fighting men was an exaggeration, as it may very well have been, when the baggage and supply trains too were counted, it was a massive force, considerably greater than any which Antony had yet commanded. Its size, as Plutarch goes on (with studied hyperbole) to say, was so great that it 'terrified even the Indians beyond Bactria and made all Asia tremble'.

Yet, in its size lay its weakness. As the mighty expedition rumbled south, its baggage carts were badly hampered by the rough terrain. So, too, the 300 lumbering ox-drawn wagons, on which the vital siege equipment was transported – equipment that included an 80-foot-long (25 metre) battering ram, essential if it should be necessary to break down a city's gates. For the impatient Antony, the painfully slow speed at which his attack force was being compelled to travel was infuriating. Caesar, he may have thought, the master of a lightning strike, would never have allowed himself to become so encumbered. Besides, such was his confidence in the sheer numbers of his troops, that he believed that shock and awe would cower the Parthians into offering surrender before a single blow was struck.

So, leaving his carts and wagons, his siege equipment and his battering ram to follow on behind him, guarded by a sizeable detachment of his troops, Antony himself with the rest of his army marched swiftly on to the wealthy city of Phraata, now the royal residence of the family of the king. If he had expected the citizens of Phraata to capitulate without a fight, he was mistaken. They closed their gates and sat tight. Antony's gamble had failed. Now, when he most needed his siege engines, he had none. All he could do was set his army to begin piling a high mound of earth against the city walls. His intention: to create a ramp up which to send his legions.

It was a thankless task (the walls were strong and well defended) and, as they were still completing it, a horseman galloped into Antony's camp with an urgent message from the baggage train. The Parthian king Phraates was attacking it. Antony must come quickly to its aid. With all haste, Antony assembled his men and together they marched back the way they had come.

The sight that met them was appalling. On the silent plain were only corpses. Of the soldiers and the drivers not a man was left alive. The carnage was complete, and there was nothing left. The baggage carts and siege engines on which Antony had realized too late that he relied, were gone. And what was more, as he learned in the days that followed, the man he thought of as his ally, Ardavastes, the Armenian king, had, at the first sign of trouble, led his men back home. His intervention might have saved the baggage train. His treachery had sealed its fate.

With seemingly no other option, Antony led his surviving troops back to Phraata and the siege. Already, even in these relatively early days of the great expedition, there were those who believed that their cause was hopeless, and, as the days dragged on, the Roman army's food supplies began to dwindle and run out. To make matters worse, King Phraates' Parthian army had arrived, and was now camped at a distance in the heat-haze of the flatlands behind Antony's own lines, menacing and still. Phraates' strategy was not to engage with the Romans, rather to hem them in and wear them down. Deep within enemy territory, the besieging army of the Romans, caught between the city and the newly arrived troops, was now itself besieged and suffering the very deprivations it had been hoping to inflict upon the Parthians.

The campaign that had begun on the Roman side as a swaggering show of strength was in danger of degenerating into a slow war of attrition, with Antony's troops bogged down in a tactical quagmire from which they would find it difficult to extract themselves. With Phraates' cataphracts, his heavily armoured cavalrymen, galloping tantalizingly close to the Roman lines and taunting them, Antony struggled to find a way to seize the initiative and engineer a situation that would compel them to give battle.

Fortunately, numbers were still on his side. Leaving a considerable force at Phraata, he struck out into the Parthian countryside with a huge army: ten legions, three cohorts of the crack praetorian guard and all his cavalry. By nightfall it seemed as if his strategy was working. Plutarch takes up the tale:

> After he had marched for one day, he realized that the Parthians were surrounding him and looking for opportunity to attack him on the road. So he displayed the flag of war inside the camp, then, striking the tents as if he meant not to fight but to retreat, he led his men past the line of barbarians, who were drawn up in a crescent formation. In fact, he had already issued orders that, as soon as the infantry were near enough to attack the enemy who were closest to them, the cavalry should launch a charge.[95]

In total silence, and maintaining the strictest discipline as if it were a military exercise and not the prelude to battle, Antony's men began the long march back to Phraata. Then, suddenly, on the given signal, their cavalry wheeled round and, peeling off from the long lines of infantry, launched their attack on the Parthians, shouting, yelling, trying to instil fear and seize the moment. The infantry now followed suit, and for an instant it seemed that Antony's tactics were working. The Parthian cataphracts were turning round their horses and spurring them to flight. The Romans were in hot pursuit. But although their cavalry kept up the chase for twenty miles (32 km), they could not catch them. The Parthians had melted into the September night. What Antony had hoped would be a famous victory had ended as an inconclusive skirmish.

The next day, he brought his army, now demoralized and no doubt questioning his leadership, back to Phraata.

> As they marched, they met at first few enemy troops, but gradually their numbers increased until finally the entire army was there, challenging and attacked them from every side, as if it was a fresh unconquered force. At last, with difficulty and after heavy fighting, the Romans reached the safety of their camp. Next the Parthians made a sortie, attacked the Romans' mound and forced its defenders to flee. Furious, Antony punished those soldiers who had been guilty of cowardice with the so-called sentence of decimation. In other words, he divided them into groups of ten and executed one man chosen by lot from each group.

In fact, the problem lay not in Roman troops. It lay in Antony. Despite his reputation, Antony had never before led an expedition of so great a size. In his early career, he had served under the competent general, Gabinius, and the inspired commander, Caesar, both of whom knew how best to utilize Antony's flamboyant energies; his own great victory at Philippi ranked as a towering success, but it owed as much to the ineptitude of the opposing generals as it did to Antony's leadership. Now, alone and exposed, Antony was floundering and his confidence was draining away.

Inevitably morale among the troops was slipping, too. Hungry men left camp to forage, never to return. Whenever Roman troops set off in greater numbers on a mission to find food, the Parthians would take advantage of the situation and attack those who remained on duty at the walls, causing as much destruction as they could, and setting fire to any siege machines the Romans managed to construct *in situ*. At the same time, Parthian cataphracts would ride close to the Roman camp at

Antony's nemesis, Phraates IV, King of the Parthians. Silver *tetradrachm* struck at Seleucia on the Tigris, 26–25 BC. Diam. 2.7 cm. British Museum, 1900,0706.62.

dusk to wage war of a much more psychological kind, praising the bravery of the Roman soldiers while pouring scorn on Antony's poor leadership.

With the autumn equinox now past and the heavy air a sign of rains and snows to come, both Antony and Phraates knew that it was time to negotiate terms for a Roman retreat. Both sides had their reasons for not wanting the situation to drag on into the winter. It was clear not only that the Romans could not win, but that Antony had no convincing strategy. Yet, knowing (as he did) the importance of appearances, Antony still saw a need to posture and to make demands.

Through envoys, he opened negotiations by stipulating that he would withdraw his army only if the Parthians returned the prisoners and eagle standards they had captured from Crassus seventeen years earlier. Unsurprisingly, Phraates was unimpressed. Ignoring Antony's demands, he launched into an expansive lecture, no doubt haranguing the envoys at length about Rome's expansionist policies from the time of Crassus down to Antony, but in the end he promised peace if they struck camp immediately and started their retreat. With no prospect of achieving any of his aims, the best that Antony could hope for was an orderly withdrawal. For a man who styled himself the new Dionysus, the ruler of the East, it was humiliating in the extreme. With one telling detail, Plutarch captures his state of mind:

> Although he could persuade a popular assembly of anything, and was better equipped than any other man of his time to inspire his troops through his eloquence, he was so consumed by shame and depression that he could not bring himself to make the usual inspiring speech to his troops.[96]

Not for the last time, Antony seemed in the grip of a debilitating depression. Without formally concluding a treaty with the Parthian king (or so it would appear), he instructed one of his lieutenants to make a rousing speech and supervise the necessary arrangements to strike camp.

Yet, any who believed their troubles to be over soon found themselves mistaken. If anything, worse suffering still lay ahead. For two days, the Roman army marched northwards to Armenia unopposed. They were following a shorter route than the one by which they had come only a few months earlier, and they believed that the terrain would offer more protection. They were wrong. On the third day, they discovered that the road ahead was flooded. The Parthians had smashed a dam, and as the Romans struggled forward they heard the terrifying thunder of approaching hooves and the metallic clattering of armour. Soon the cataphracts were galloping around them, sending volley after volley of their arrows into the midst of the retreating Romans. Antony's Celtic cavalry charged out against them, and for the time being the Parthians withdrew. But the truth was clear. Far from allowing them safe passage home, the enemy were bent on causing as much carnage as they could.

The historian Dio Cassius paints a vivid picture of the retreat:

> [The Romans] wandered into unfamiliar country and became lost. Meanwhile, the barbarians occupied the passes before the Romans could reach them, blocking them with trenches or barricades. They also made it difficult to get water from anywhere, and at the same time destroyed the crops; and if (by chance) the Romans' march seemed about to take them into easier countryside, the Parthians would cause them to turn aside with false accounts that these areas were already under enemy control. As a result, the Romans took different routes, which led them into roadside ambushes, and many died either as a result of this or through starvation. This led to desertions. In fact, they would all have changed sides, had it not been for the fact that those who did desert were shot by the barbarians in full view of the rest of the Roman army.[97]

To protect the men and animals, the Romans retreated in a hollow square, a formation called the *testudo* or 'tortoise'. Again, Dio's description is vivid:

> Baggage animals, light-armed troops and cavalry are stationed in the centre of the army, while drawn up on the outside in a rectangular formation are the heavily armed infantry with their oblong, curved, and cylindrical shields. These face outwards and, weapons at the ready, they surround the others. The men in the centre, equipped with flat shields, form a tight mass, holding their shields above their own heads and the heads of all the others, so that nothing except shields can be seen across the entire formation, and, thanks to the solidity of the formation, everyone is protected from missiles. It is so remarkably strong that men can walk on top of it, and even horses and vehicles can be driven over it, should they come to a tight gully . . .[98]

Yet, to march in such a tight formation over such unforgiving ground meant to make slow and painful progress, especially in such rugged mountainous terrain as now confronted them. Time and again the Parthian cataphracts launched their attacks, unleashing their deadly deluges of arrows on the struggling Romans. On one occasion at least, the shame of the retreat caused officers to disregard their orders and seek to engage the enemy. The legions involved were surrounded and cut off. Only with difficulty could reinforcements reach them, and by the end of the engagement three thousand of their men lay dead. Five thousand more had been injured.

For the most part, however, discipline held. Once, as they were struggling down a mountainside under fierce fire from the enemy, the Romans drew on years of training to execute a dazzling manoeuvre:

> The infantry with their oblong shields wheeled around to enclose the light-armed troops. Then the first rank dropped on one knee, their shields held out in front of them. The second rank held their shields over the heads of the first and the rank behind repeated the manoeuvre. This formation looks very like a tiled roof, and, while looking rather theatrical, is a most effective defence against arrows, which simply bounce off it. But the Parthians interpreted the sight of the Romans dropping on to one knee, as a sign that they were exhausted, so they put down their bows, took tight hold of their spears and advanced to close quarters. At this, the Romans shouted the war-cry and suddenly sprang to their feet, lunging forward with their javelins. They slaughtered the the Parthian front line and routed the rest.[99]

With such a combination of tactics, bravery and dogged perseverance, Antony and his Romans made their harrowing retreat, avoiding the great plains where (they had been warned) the great bulk of the Parthian army lay in wait, and clinging to the icy mountain tracks. With food largely unavailable, soldiers ate whatever they could find. Once, grasses infected with a poison fungus caused many who ate them to hallucinate and vomit, still more to die. Another time, drinking brackish water brought on dysentery.

By the time they had been marching for three weeks, hounded and harried constantly, plagued by the cold, worn down by thirst and hunger, some among the men had had enough. Riots broke out within the camp. Looters made off with gold and silver from their fellow soldiers' packs. Antony's own baggage train was pillaged. It was a low point in an already miserable adventure. Perhaps not for the first time, Antony contemplated suicide.

Yet, in the morning, discipline restored, the Romans beat off a fresh attack and slowly edged towards a fast-flowing river. As they made their crossing, they began to realize that they were no longer under fire. The Parthians had unstrung their bows. Praising the Romans' bravery, they announced that the army could cross over without fear. Within five days, still vigilant but not attacked, Antony and his exhausted men had reached another river, the Araxes, the border with Armenia, and safety. The soldiers 'kissed the earth and embraced one another with tears of happiness, like sailors who had just caught sight of land'.[100] The Parthian campaign was over.

It had been an unmitigated disaster. Antony had achieved none of his objectives. The eagle standards lost by Crassus were still in the Parthians' hands; with them the Roman prisoners of war. Moreover, far from enhancing Rome's prestige among her enemies, all that the offensive had achieved was to expose her vulnerability. Perhaps as many as a third of those who had set out some six or seven months before had lost their lives, either in the fighting or in the calamitous retreat.

As for Antony himself, his standing among his men remained unshaken. Speaking of the troops he led, Plutarch is at pains to emphasize

> the respect that his men felt for him as general, their obedience and goodwill. Every one of them – those of high standing, those of none; officers and men alike – shared one common consent, that they held Antony's respect and goodwill in higher esteem than their own lives and safety.[101]

Even on this ill-starred expedition

> by sharing in their suffering and their distress, and by giving each man what he needed, he caused the sick and injured to be even more eager to serve him than those who were fit and well.

Among Antony's enemies, however, a different view took hold. In Rome, there was a faction which was all too ready to heap scorn on Antony for his handling of the Parthian campaign. And among those heaping scorn there was a growing number, shaking their censorious heads, pointing their accusing fingers, muttering that Antony had rendered the whole expedition useless from the start

> because of Cleopatra. For so impatient was he to spend the winter with her that he began the campaign before he was ready and conducted it chaotically. He was no longer in control of his own judgement, but like the victim of a drug or magic spell, his gaze was always drawn to her and his mind more concerned about his quick return to her than about conquering the enemy.[102]

A Roman army on campaign crosses a river in a relief from Trajan's Column in Rome, dedicated in AD 113.

It was a malicious charge, yet Antony did little to dispel it. Indeed, rather than overwinter in Armenia, he had already begun the long march back west towards the Mediterranean coast. In shocking weather and in bitter cold, the driving, drifting snow slowing down the progress of already fatigued men, the remnants of the Roman army battled against the elements to make their slow way back to Syria and to their winter quarters. Eight thousand more men perished on the march. They had survived the Parthians only to die from the winter cold and Antony's desire to strike back west.

Once back in Syria, Antony left his troops and, accompanied by only his closest retinue, rode to a tiny harbour called White Village, 'Leuke Kome'. He had already sent an urgent message south to Alexandria for

Cleopatra to come here to join him. Yet, when he reached the shore, save for a few poor fishing boats, the harbour was empty. Dismayed by his failures, distressed by the horrors that, through his own miscalculations, his army had endured, despondent and depressed, Antony needed the support of Cleopatra now as never before. Holed up in the storm-lashed village, his nerves reached breaking point. Every day he expected Cleopatra; every day she did not come.

He was distraught and quickly gave himself over to drinking and drunkenness. Yet even at table he could not settle, but he would often jump up with a drink in his hand and run outside to see if she was coming.[103]

Nervous and increasingly paranoid, he must have started questioning just what had happened in his absence and wondering if, now that he had conceded so much territory and power to the Egyptian queen, and now that he had himself been humiliated so spectacularly, Cleopatra had decided to abandon him.

CHAPTER 8

Two Against the World

THE WHITE VILLAGE: WINTER 36–35 BC

FOR WEEKS, ANTONY GAZED out across the empty sea, the long waves rolling in, rank after rank, to break in a cold spume of foam against the stone wall of the harbour. With every day that Cleopatra failed to come, his mood turned blacker. Not only was he haunted by the horrors of his failed campaign to Parthia and the disastrous retreat; what news he now received from Rome of Octavian's successes served only to heighten his own sense of personal catastrophe.

For, in the past year, the tectonic plates of politics in Rome had shifted once again, and a new world order was emerging. Of great significance had been Octavian's two victories over Sextus Pompey, whose control of Sicily's rich corn fields had been threatening the safe supply of food to Rome itself. Now, thanks to the brilliance of Octavian's admiral, Marcus Agrippa, Pompey's fleet, for so long seemingly invincible, had been smashed, Pompey himself was on the run and Octavian was lording it in Rome.

As well he might. It was not only Pompey's power he had destroyed. In the weeks following Agrippa's victories, the third triumvir, Lepidus, had tried to flex his muscles too. War seemed inevitable. But in an uncharacteristic act of bravery, Octavian himself rode into Lepidus' camp and urged his legions to come over to his side. They did. War was avoided, Lepidus deposed, and now, instead of three commanders, the Roman Empire had but two: Octavian and Antony.

There was no doubt whose star was more in the ascendant. While Antony had been suffering humiliating losses far away in Parthia, Octavian had been not only winning victories but also consolidating his own power base back in Rome. For Romans, Rome was where it mattered. Success in Parthia would have brought Antony great kudos. Failure, even if in his dispatches Antony did try to hide its true extent, not only handed ammunition to his enemies in Rome but also lessened his standing in the eyes of his own soldiers and supporters in the East. It was not a situation Antony was used to.

The luxuriant Dionysus, Antony's patron god. Cast bronze head, originally a support for a handle on a bronze vessel (*situla*). Roman, c.200–100 BC. Height 21.4 cm. British Museum, 1989,0130.1, purchased with contribution from the National Heritage Memorial Fund.

Silver *denarius* showing Antony (obverse, top) and Cleopatra (reverse), struck at a travelling mint, 32 BC. Diam. 1.85 cm. British Museum, TC,p237.2. CleMA.

At last, though, on the far horizon, at first almost a mirage, then slowly more substantial, the linen sails of the Egyptian fleet appeared, and among them the purple sails of the royal flagship. For Antony, the long and agonizing wait was over. Not only had Cleopatra braved the winter waves to come to him in person, she had brought with her supplies of food and clothing for his troops and desperately needed funds. Now, even if he had to use some of his own and of his friends' resources to augment what Cleopatra brought, he could reward his men and buy back their precarious loyalty:

> Each infantrymen received four hundred sesterces, with an appropriate sum going to the rest. In fact, the amount sent was insufficient, so Antony made up the remainder from his own funds, and although he bore the expense himself he still gave Cleopatra the credit for her generosity; he required his friends, too, to make large contributions and levied large amounts from his allies.[104]

Cash and comestibles were perhaps not all that Cleopatra brought to the White Village. Perhaps she also brought the young son, Ptolemy, still only a few months old, conceived in Antioch in what, to Antony, must already have seemed another age. Perhaps to Cleopatra, too. In the wake of his defeat, and after weeks of heavy, maudlin drinking, Antony must have appeared a seriously altered man. Cleopatra's own assessment of his state of mind is not recorded, but within weeks, if not days, she had extracted him from the lonely isolation of the Syrian coast and was sailing with him back to his beloved Alexandria. Here, if anywhere, she could help him recuperate and regain his legendary *joie de vivre*.

She was not, however, the only woman to have designs on coming to Antony's aid. Before long (spring 35 BC), news came that his wife, Octavia, had arrived in Athens. With her she had brought men, money and supplies to aid her husband in his war against the Parthians. Or so, at the time, it seemed. A century or so later, Plutarch, writing with the benefit of hindsight, thought it was all a ruse, a pretext in a time of troubles, to feed the flames of conflict. According to him,

> most people agree that the reason Octavian permitted her to do this was not to please her, but to give himself a plausible pretext for war, if she should be rebuffed or insulted by Antony.[105]

He goes on to paint a compelling picture of a war by proxy, in which Octavia and Cleopatra each fight to win control of Antony: Octavia, the loyal Roman wife, sending dignified and measured messages inviting her husband to join her in Athens; Cleopatra resorting to wiles, theatricality and emotional blackmail to keep him ensconced in Alexandria. If Plutarch's account is clouded by propaganda, it is propaganda Octavian's men were undoubtedly already beginning to disseminate. It tells (with unashamed hyperbole) how Cleopatra

> behaved as if she herself was consumed with desire for Antony; she ate very little; she lost a lot of weight; she looked longingly at Antony whenever he came near her; she appeared faint and downcast whenever he left. She did her best to make sure that she was often observed to be weeping, and then quickly to wipe her tears away and try to conceal them as if she wished to hide her grief from Antony . . . Her sycophants, too, were busy on her behalf, rebuking Antony for being insensitive and cold, a man who would destroy a woman who was utterly devoted to him and him alone. Octavia, they said, had married him for politics and the sake of her brother's interests, and she enjoyed the status of a wife: but Cleopatra, queen of so many people, bore the name of mistress merely – not that she rejected the title or thought it beneath her, as long as she could see him and spend her life with him; but she could not go on living if he discarded her.

This version of the facts, where a vacillating Antony is manipulated by a scheming Cleopatra, was to become engrained in Roman popular belief to such an overwhelming extent that it is now impossible to tease out truth from counter-information. There were undoubtedly good reasons why Antony did not rush headlong to Octavia in Athens. For one thing, the troops which she had brought from her brother were less than Octavian had promised Antony some years before; for another, Antony was already receiving reports from Parthia of a schism, which, if he were to move fast, he could well exploit to his military advantage.

But before he could make any sort of move, either north to Athens or east against Parthia, urgent news arrived which he could not ignore. The fugitive Sextus Pompey had landed on the shores of Asia and was recruiting a new army. Before long, his envoys were turning up in Alexandria. Their message was blunt but clear. Just as in the aftermath of the Perusine War (see p. 98) Pompey pledged his full support to Antony – for a war against Octavian. Addressing Antony, they told him:

You are now all that stands between Octavian and the sole command he so desires. If it were not for Pompey, he would be at war with you already. You probably could see this for yourself, but Pompey brings it to your notice through goodwill to you, since he prefers a man who is blameless and magnanimous to one who is deceitful, treacherous and devious.[106]

For a moment, perhaps, Antony was undecided, but within days other envoys from Pompey arrived at the Alexandrian royal palace, this time under armed guard. They had been caught and arrested trying to smuggle messages offering support to Phraates, King of Parthia. Pompey had been playing a double game. If Antony did not embrace him, he would go over to Rome's bitterest enemy.

Pompey had sealed his own fate. Desperately, he led his army inland. His goal, it was said, was Armenia, and the court of the same King Artavasdes who had failed so disastrously to help Antony in Parthia the year before. But before he got there, he was intercepted by Antony's forces, taken into custody and brought back to the sea-board city of Miletus, where, on the orders of Antony, he was executed. He was the last surviving rebel general from the civil war between his father, Gnaeus Pompey, and Caesar, making it all the more ironic that, even as his body was being laid out for its burial, the seeds of the next Roman civil war, already germinating for so many years, were now ripe for their sprouting.

By the time of Pompey's death in 35 BC, the year was too far gone for Antony to contemplate campaigning. By letter, he had already conveyed his wish that his wife Octavia should return to Rome. No doubt he heard how, on her arrival, Octavian her brother had told her to divorce Antony, advising her

A false friend, Artavasdes II (56–31 BC), shown here on a silver *drachm*, was seized by Antony and executed by Cleopatra. The coin was minted at Artaxata in Armenia. Diam. 1.7 cm. British Museum, 1872,0709.327.

to return to her own house. But she said she would not leave her husband's house; in fact, she begged Octavian that, if he had not already decided to declare war for other reasons, he should overlook Antony's treatment of her, for it would be shameful to have it said that their two most powerful commanders had plunged the Roman people into civil war, one out of passion for a woman, the other out of indignation on a woman's behalf.[107]

Again Plutarch, who tells the story, writes from hindsight, yet he must surely capture accurately the mood of the day. For, if there was any doubt that war was in the air, it was diminishing with every month that passed, and with his defeat in Parthia still hanging over him, Antony needed to restore morale – and quickly.

So, with the beginning of the campaigning season the next year (34 BC), Antony rejoined his army and marched out against an enemy whom he had every reason to despise: Artavasdes, King of Armenia. Not only had Artavasdes betrayed Antony in Parthia, he had connived with Sextus Pompey; and, besides, he was an easy target. In fact, the war took little fighting. Artavasdes was defeated not by force but by deception, and his kingdom claimed for Rome. As victories went, it was far from spectacular, but a victory it was nonetheless, and for Antony that was enough. His spirits restored to their former stratospheric heights, he turned his horse's head for Alexandria and a dazzling celebration.

It was to be one of the most extravagant spectacles which the Ptolemaic capital had ever witnessed, a celebration of victory, a display of power, a carnival, a pageant stretching over many days and embracing the whole city. By the early morning, with the rising sun already bathing the limestone pillars of the colonnades and throwing the pink and green facades of buildings into sharper focus, the route along the wide Canopic Boulevard was lined with expectant citizens – for they knew that they were about to witness a sight more redolent of Rome than of the Egyptian capital. They would not be disappointed.

West from the Canopic Gate, the first of the procession came into view, and soon the captives taken in Armenia were shuffling disconsolately in chains rank upon sullen rank along the broad and airy boulevard. Interspersed at times, no doubt, were floats, some laden down with booty, others perhaps showing models of Armenian towns, but behind them all came the greatest prize of all: King Artavasdes and his family, bound in golden chains, a royal humiliation. Then, riding in a golden chariot, 'his head crowned with ivy, his body swathed in a saffron cloth of gold, and in his hand a thyrsus',[108] came Antony himself, the embodiment of Dionysus, patron god of all the East.

As he rode up the wide boulevard, the cheers not only of the Alexandrians but of his Roman troops, too, ringing in his ears, with flower-buds showered on him by well-wishers and petals dancing in the warm salt air, Antony could see ahead of him Queen Cleopatra 'in the midst of all her people', raised on a silver-plated dais and seated on a golden throne. Egypt had played its part in the Armenian victory; now Antony was honouring her with its spoils.

The symbolism of the whole event was clear. Dressed as he was as Dionysus, the god whom Greeks and Romans called the 'Liberator', and with whom generations of past Ptolemaic kings had been identified, Antony was using this triumphal bacchic procession to cement his own position in the minds of his Eastern subjects and allies. God and Ptolemy: he now was both. And just as the city's founder, Alexander, had ruled vast tracts of the East, where myth said Dionysus had once journeyed, so Antony would show that his sway, too, extended just as far. Arch-impresario that he was, Antony knew the importance of appearance, and with war-clouds massing on the western horizon it was particularly vital now to expunge any memories of the disasters in Parthia and eclipse them with a shameless show of his dominion over all the East. The way he chose to demonstrate this dominion stretched even his theatrical imagination to the limits.

The vast gymnasium at Alexandria, with its colonnades two hundred metres long, was turned into a massive auditorium. There was space enough for many thousand onlookers, citizenry, soldiers, courtiers, ambassadors, and at its heart, the focus of the whole great multitude, was erected a high platform walled with silver. On it were six thrones: two were tall and made of gold, the others, smaller, less ornate, nestled at their feet. As expectancy grew palpable, and to a flurry of brash pomp, there entered onto the stage the sextet, whom onlookers could have been excused for calling the Egyptian royal family.

How Antony was dressed we do not know. Perhaps he was again arrayed as Dionysus. At his side was Cleopatra, in her role as Isis, with her black robes and her crown. And around them the royal children: the thirteen-year-old Caesarion; the six-year-old twins Cleopatra Selene and Alexander Helios, the latter dressed in full Median regalia and crowned with a tiara and an upright turban; and Ptolemy Philadelphus, not yet two years old, costumed in the finery of a Macedonian king in boots, a short cloak and a woollen hat encircled by a diadem.

When the others had been seated, Antony, the orator, raised his right hand in the familiar gesture and began his speech. Its sheer audacity was breathtaking.

> First he declared Cleopatra Queen of Egypt, Cyprus, Libya and Coele Syria, along with her co-ruler Caesarion . . . Next he proclaimed his own sons by Cleopatra 'Kings of Kings'. To Alexander he assigned Armenia, Media and Parthia (when conquered), and to Ptolemy Phoenicia, Syria and Cilicia . . . The boys embraced their parents, after which Alexander was given an honour-guard of Armenians, and Ptolemy an honour-guard of Macedonians.[109]

As a piece of showmanship these so-called Donations of Alexandria were unrivalled. As a political settlement, however, it was and remains quite baffling. Not only were certain lands (like Parthia) as yet unconquered, most of the others were not Antony's to give. True, his position as one of the two remaining triumvirs gave him enormous power, but the expectation was that he would use this power for the good of Rome, not to donate

Rome's territories to Egyptian queens and princes. But Rome was no longer Antony's prime audience. His power-base was in the East, in countries used to monarchy. Ten years before, Antony had offered Caesar a crown; now he was setting one on his own head. If, as seemed likely, war with Octavian was unavoidable, Antony, as king and Dionysus, would use all his powers of propaganda to rally his forces to him.

In Rome the news of Antony's 'donations' enjoyed a mixed reception. His friends were horrified. Two of them, both consuls for the year, deliberately prevented Antony's despatches describing the event from being read out in public, so much did they fear the repercussions. Octavian, on the other hand, was delighted. This was precisely the kind of behaviour that would alienate Antony from Rome and help provide an excuse for war. What was the procession through the streets of Alexandria, after all, if not 'a kind of triumph'?[110] And triumphs, as any Roman knew, must take place in Rome, the heart of empire, the rightful recipient of prisoners and booty – not in barbarian Egypt. Surely Antony had been bewitched by Cleopatra. Not only had he shunned Octavia, his lawful wife; he had rejected Rome.

In private, too, Octavian appears to have expressed concern to Antony, not only as a fellow-triumvir but also as a brother-in-law. A century or so later, the biographer Suetonius found a letter said to be in Antony's own hand kept in the imperial archives at Rome. Clearly a response to a plea from Octavian that Antony should moderate his behaviour, its style is shockingly blunt and confrontational:

> Why have you changed? Because I'm screwing the queen? She's my wife. And is this some new affair or has it been going on for nine years? And you – are you screwing only Livia? Hurrah, if when you read this letter you have not been screwing Tertulla or Terentilla, Rufilla or Salvia Titiseniam or all of them. What does it matter where or in whom you stick your erection?[111]

Many have tried to apologize for this letter – not for its tone, but for the third of its sentences. Attempts have been made to turn it into a question – 'is she my wife?' – but this is to stretch the Latin to breaking point. Others have taken the statement seriously and tried to prove an actual marriage between Antony and Cleopatra, but there is no evidence of such a ceremony, even though it would have provided strong ammunition to their enemies. In fact, the letter is a challenge, not simply from one leader to another, but from man to man, from Antony the seasoned old campaigner to the despised Octavian. It is a personal insult, a gauntlet thrown down, and as such it is far from subtle.

At the same time as Octavian was working publicly to impose a new moral gravity in Rome, in Alexandria Antony and Cleopatra appeared to be doing their best to flaunt their louche and lavish lifestyles, while members of Antony's personal retinue were benefiting from the bestowal of significant economic concessions. Stories filtered back to Rome of luxurious banquets. At one, it was rumoured, Cleopatra had responded to a wager from Antony that she could not spend 10,000,000 sesterces on one meal by dissolving a priceless pearl, one of her earrings, in strong vinegar and drinking it.

> When Cleopatra was getting ready to destroy the other pearl, too, in the same way Lucius Plancus, who was adjudicating, placed his hand on it, and declared that Antony had lost the bet.[112]

At another, it was said, this same Lucius Plancus, Antony's private secretary, had

Cleopatra is said to have dissolved a priceless pearl earring such as this for a bet. Gold earring with two pearls and two beads. 3rd century AD. Height 3.3 cm. British Museum, 1917,0601.2672, bequeathed by Augustus Wollaston Franks.

> performed the role of Glaucus the Nereid, dancing naked, with his body painted blue, his head crowned with reeds, wearing a fish tail and writhing about on his knees.[113]

In time, such fun grew stale even for Plancus. Within eighteen months (32 BC) he had slipped out of Antony's household and scuttled back to Rome, where, parading his loathing of Cleopatra, he began to spread malicious stories about his former friend and colleague. Most dangerous of them all concerned Antony's will, a copy of which had been deposited for safe-keeping with the Vestal Virgins. In the propaganda war, this will was gold dust. Flouting the very traditions he claimed to uphold, Octavian requisitioned it and (like Antony a decade earlier when he used Caesar's will to whip up public indignation against the assassins) gleefully read from it both in the Senate House and in a public assembly. According to Octavian, one of the clauses of the will stipulated that Antony's body should be buried by Cleopatra's side in Alexandria.

Without sight of the document, it is impossible to know how much Octavian embroidered or even altered what Antony himself had written, but certainly its reading served to fan the flames of public indignation. Already Rome was rife with tittle-tattle about heinous deeds in the East. Antony's un-Roman behaviour was, so conservative Italians whispered, a sign that Cleopatra had bewitched him. Encouraged by Octavian and his agents, men muttered in real or contrived horror how

Antony sometimes wore a short eastern sword in his belt, dressed in foreign clothing, and could be seen even in public lying on a gilded couch or sitting in a chair of similar description. He was portrayed alongside Cleopatra in paintings and statues, where he was said to represent Osiris or Dionysus and she Selene or Isis. Thanks especially to this he seemed to have been bewitched by her through magic.[114]

But more pernicious were the claims that

Cleopatra beguiled and captivated not just Antony but anyone else who had any influence on him so much that she began to entertain the hope of ruling the Romans, too; and whenever she swore an oath, the most powerful phrase she used to swear by was her intention to dispense justice from the Capitol.[115]

As the war of words escalated, Antony began to make more concrete preparations for a military clash with Octavian. The year after the theatricalities of the 'Donations of Alexandria', Antony transferred his legions from the banks of the Euphrates (where they had been mustered prior to an attack on Parthia) back to the Ionian coast of Asia Minor (33 BC). In the current climate, when the real adversary was within the empire's frontiers, this was no time to be far off in the distant East, doing battle with external enemies.

Meanwhile, as Octavian manoeuvred ever more insidiously and successfully against him in the Senate back in Rome, Antony with Cleopatra by his side cruised with two hundred warships from Alexandria up the western coast of Asia Minor to the rich and elegant port city of Ephesus. Here in the great bay, its coast bejewelled with gleaming marble towns and studded with rich villas, the military force was being assembled. Eight hundred ships in all were dragged up onto slipways to be overhauled and strengthened for the coming conflict, while soldiers from sixteen legions, perhaps 80,000 men, were drilled for battle. At the same time, quartermasters stalked through warehouses, piled ever higher with supplies, and, on the banks of the River Caister beneath the heights of Mount Koressos, traders and camp followers set up encampments.

No doubt there was time to visit the magnificent temple of Artemis, its gleaming walls, twenty metres high, adorned with works of art already centuries old, its columns cased in gold and silver, their bases carved exquisitely with scenes from Greek mythology, its echoing interior the home to the mysterious cult statue of Artemis of Ephesus, her breast adorned with many bulls' testicles, her coloured robes stitched with the twelve signs of the zodiac, her arms outstretched to embrace her worshippers. As Cleopatra climbed the temple steps she may have felt a momentary chill as she thought perhaps of the ghost of her sister Arsinoë, slaughtered there on her command just eight years earlier.

But soon concerns of a more substantial kind occupied her mind. Some of Antony's generals were already becoming increasingly unhappy about Cleopatra's presence at Ephesus. Partly this must have been due to chauvinistic Roman beliefs that warfare was a male preserve, but partly it may have been prompted by her somewhat imperious personality. Although she could be diplomatic when she needed to, it was not unknown for Cleopatra to be brutally direct in her dealings with men who were unused to the condescension of monarchs and believed that they deserved better.

It says much about the dynamics of their relationship that, while Antony listened to his advisers and urged Cleopatra to return to Egypt, the queen refused to go. Publicly, her reasons were 'that it was unfair to send from the theatre of war a woman who had contributed so many resources to it, and unwise for Antony to undermine the morale of the Egyptians who formed such a large part of their naval force'.[116]

Privately, however, after the debacle of his expedition to Parthia and the mental anguish he suffered in its aftermath, Cleopatra may well have been reluctant to place all her trust in Antony's powers of command. Besides, she had learned much at first hand from the great Caesar, not least that a leader must be where the action is. Not that this was what she told Antony. Rather, she persuaded a confidante to remind him that it was thanks to 'her long association with Antony that she had learned to manage important business'.

As important as command, materiel and men, were the perceptions of the cities of the East. The next spring (32 BC), Antony proclaimed a lavish Festival of Dionysus to be held on the vine-clad island of Samos, a few miles across the strait north of Ephesus. It was perhaps his most concerted effort yet to establish himself as the embodiment of Dionysus, a godlike leader around whom his troops might rally. Perhaps he believed, too, that he might gain the favour of the god himself. Thanks to Octavian's deliberate campaign of misinformation, even near contemporary writers dismissed the festival as mere frivolity, but Plutarch's account does contain a hint of Antony's true purpose:

> For just all the kings, princes, tetrarchs, nations and cities between Syria and the Mareotic Lake, Armenia and Illyria had been ordered to bring or send equipment for the war, so all the Actors of Dionysus were commanded to come to Samos. So, while virtually all the world surrounding them was filled with groans and lamentations, this one island reverberated for many days with the music of flutes and stringed instruments; the theatres were full; the choruses vied one

with another. Each city sent an ox for public sacrifice, and the kings in Antony's entourage competed to provide the most magnificent offerings and entertainments. And so the word went round, 'How will they celebrate their victory, if they celebrate so lavishly before the war has yet begun?' When the festival was over, Antony gave the Actors of Dionysus the city of Priene as their home, while he sailed on to Athens.

Only six years earlier, Antony had overwintered in Athens with his new wife Octavia, with whom he had been infatuated (see p. 102). Now, from the same city, he sent agents back to Rome with instructions to evict her from his house. Brutal and insensitive his orders may have been, but their main aim was to goad Octavian.

Not that Octavian needed goading. Already, he had imposed a war tax throughout Italy. Its rate (twelve and a half per cent on property owned by freedmen and a crippling twenty-five per cent on that owned by citizens) provoked riots, but with Antony's army massing only 350 miles from the Italian coast, Octavian now needed to respond with all the speed he could. For, although a war of words had been raging for some years, no one in Rome had believed that Antony would ratchet up hostilities so quickly – especially as until relatively recently, when not preoccupied with Alexandria, such attention as he gave to war seemed to have been entirely focused on Armenia and Parthia.

Had Antony struck quickly and shipped his army over to Brundisium, he would have found an Italy woefully unprepared and in internal crisis. But he did not. Loath to bring civil war on to the shores of his native Italy, he remained for almost all that year in Athens with Cleopatra (32 BC). There was much about the city which appealed to him, not least the ancient sanctuary of Dionysus nestling in the shadow of the gleaming acropolis, with its temple and its theatre, one of the earliest and certainly the most evocative in all the Roman world. For it was here that imperial Athens had paraded her spoils of war four centuries before (5th century BC). Here, too, the great dramas of Aeschylus, Sophocles and Euripides had been staged, masterpieces which themselves had influenced much Roman literature.

Yet now even the plots of these same Greek tragedies were being used by his enemies to belittle Antony. Some of the dramas had shown Hercules, enslaved to Omphale, an Eastern queen, and so bewitched by her that he gave her his lion-skin and club, while he himself dressed in women's clothes and helped her spin wool. For Octavian's supporters the parallels were rib-ticklingly neat, especially as Antony claimed to trace his ancestry to Hercules. In Italy, zealously pro-Octavian painters began to depict the myth on vases.

It was such a convenient spin: the exotic foreign woman, Cleopatra, had cast a spell on the true Roman, Antony. As the months went by, more and more reports came out of Athens that (conveniently for Octavian) served to bolster the already xenophobic and misogynistic preconceptions of Rome's elders. They told of how Antony

Dedicated to Dionysus, the slope above the theatre at Athens was once the site of a Dionysiac gazebo in which Antony and his friends had partied from early morning.

> had made a gift to [Cleopatra] of the libraries at Pergamum, in which there were 200,000 complete books; at a banquet attended by many guests, he had stood up and rubbed her feet, to honour some agreement they had made; … often, when he was seated on the tribunal, dispensing justice to tetrarchs and kings, he would receive and read love-letters from her, written on tablets of onyx or crystal. On one occasion when Furnius (a very distinguished man, the greatest orator in Rome) was speaking, Cleopatra was carried through the Agora (market-place) in her litter. When Antony saw her, he jumped up from his tribunal, abandoned the trial and went off with her, hanging onto her litter.[117]

Even Plutarch, our source for these allegations, believes they were invented. Indeed, their details seem to be deliberately chosen to excite true Roman wrath, from the surrender of the library at Pergamum (which had been among the first overseas settlements bequeathed to the people of Rome) to the love-letters written on tablets of onyx or crystal (real Romans would eschew such Eastern *luxuria*) to Antony's shunning of the distinguished Roman Furnius, preferring to hang off Cleopatra's litter like some love-struck boy.

It was all so very different from the home life of Octavian – or so his propaganda went. While the middle-aged Antony was doting on Cleopatra, young Octavian was a beacon of traditional morality. While Antony was giving away whole tracts of hard-won empire, Octavian was rebuilding Rome, transforming the once shambolic city into a truly imperial capital. While Antony was planning for a burial in far-off Alexandria, Octavian had already ordered the construction of a mausoleum by the Tiber near the heart of his native Rome. The contrast was clear for anyone to see. Octavian was trying to bolster Rome, Antony to destroy it.

Of course, the fact that many of our sources for these years are clearly based on propagandists hostile to Antony and Cleopatra does not mean that we should dismiss everything they say. Clearly there were those with them in Athens at the time who were unhappy with the course events were taking. Over the months, an increasing number of Antony's once loyal supporters began to feel sufficiently alienated that they packed their bags, left Athens and declared allegiance to Octavian. Almost every one of them brought his own story: from Plancus, who had found Cleopatra's behaviour insulting and who advised Octavian to read Antony's will (see above), to Dellius, once one of Antony's most trusted lieutenants, who accused Cleopatra of trying to poison him.

Even Antony's friends in Rome found that they received short shrift when they attempted to advise him about Octavian's political manoeuvring:

> They sent one of their people, Geminius, to beg Antony not to let himself be voted out of office and declared an enemy of Rome. But when Geminius reached Greece, Cleopatra suspected him of being an agent of Octavia, so he was constantly humiliated with cutting jokes and by being seated in the lowest place at table. Geminius put up with all this and waited for his chance to speak to Antony. But one evening at dinner he was asked to tell why he had come, and he replied that, although the rest of what he had to say required a more sober occasion, there was one thing that he knew whether he was drunk or sober, and that was that all would be well if Cleopatra

was sent packing back to Egypt. Antony was outraged, but Cleopatra said: 'Well done, Geminius, to confess the truth without having to be tortured.' A few days later, Geminius escaped and went back to Rome.[118]

The next time messengers arrived from Italy, their news was altogether grimmer. Like Antony, Octavian had been unwilling to provoke what would appear to be a civil war against a fellow Roman general. Now events and his own propaganda had furnished him with a much more acceptable alternative.

As a young man many years before, Octavian had presided over the flummery of the pseudo-Trojan Games, when Caesar had held his four triumphs to mark the ending of his war with Pompey (46 BC). Now, as the leader of the Western empire, in the late summer of 32 BC, Octavian had resurrected (or invented) another ancient ritual, but this time with more ominous intent. Wearing his military cloak, he had gone with his entourage out onto the Field of Mars to the temple of Bellona, the harsh goddess of war. Outside its doors, in his role as presiding priest, Octavian himself had cut the throat of a sacrificial beast, and in its warm black blood had dipped a spear-point. Then, taking careful aim, he had hurled the weapon over a squat column, which, although of no great size, was yet of huge significance. For it marked the boundary of a special area of ground, already ceremonially designated as representing foreign soil. On this day the soil it symbolized was Egypt's. As the blooded spear-head thudded deep into the earth, and its shaft cast its dark shadow across the Field of Mars, all who were there to witness it knew what it portended. Rome was at war. But not with Antony. With Cleopatra.

CHAPTER 9

Battle Circus

ACTIUM, GREECE: 2 SEPTEMBER 31 BC

IN THE LONG MONTHS SINCE WAR had been officially declared, events had assumed a new momentum of their own. In Alexandria and Athens, news of Octavian's declaration of hostilities must have come as no surprise, though some tacticians may have questioned its timing. For not only were Octavian's coffers still notoriously empty, his troops were not in place, and, with the approach of autumn, the sea-lanes (so essential for transporting men and munitions) were becoming increasingly unreliable. Time seemed to be on Antony's side. A measured, leisurely response seemed not unreasonable.

So, rejecting any advice he may have received to seize the initiative and launch a lightning attack on Italy, Antony instead ordered the relocation of both his fleet and legions forward to the western coast of Greece and to the islands stippling the shores of the Ionian Sea. Here, in a long chain of ports and bays and fishing villages, from Methone at the south-west tip of the Peloponnese to Corfu in the north, his troops would overwinter, their presence a wall of bristling weaponry to deter invasion and protect the east. By far the greatest numbers were concentrated in the great Gulf of Ambracia, where a narrow channel, a mere 700 metres across, protected a lagoon some 40 kilometres long and 15 wide, a natural safe haven against the ravages of winter.

With his troops in place and his supply lines secure, Antony settled into winter quarters of his own in the ancient port of Patrae, which nestled on a fertile strip of land between the mountains and the sea. With him was Cleopatra. Here, surrounded by their generals and courtiers and flatterers, they distributed largesse, minting jingoistic coins, and sending coffers crammed with gold and silver across the sea to Italy to bolster their support.

In Rome itself, Octavian, still desperately preparing for the coming spring, responded by ratcheting up his propaganda campaign. At such a time of crisis, the significance of almost anything out of the ordinary was recorded and debated. Thus Dio tells us:

Marcus Agrippa, Octavian's brilliant admiral, veils his head for sacrifice. Marble portrait statue, c.25–10 BC. Found on Capri. Height 43 cm. British Museum, 1873,0820.730.

A monkey got in to the Temple of Demeter [Ceres], causing total mayhem; an eagle-owl flew first into the temple of Concord, and then into almost every one of the most holy shrines ... The ceremonial chariot of Jupiter, which was kept in the Roman Hippodrome [Circus], was shattered, and for days on end a flaming light rose above the horizon and shot high into the sky across the sea in the direction of Greece.[119]

Much more useful to Octavian, however, were unusual events with a clear and unequivocal meaning, like the 'impromptu' play fight between two groups of children pretending to be his army and that of Antony. 'They fought for two days, and in the end the Antony's side was defeated.' How convenient for the morale of Octavian's real troops! Then there were omens from elsewhere across the Roman world:

Honouring his legions, Antony struck coins like this one (to the Eighteenth Legion) in the winter of 32–31 BC. Silver *denarius*, struck at a travelling mint. Diam. 1.85 cm. British Museum, R.9494, donated by King George IV.

Pisaurum, a city colonized by Antony near the Adriatic Sea, was swallowed up by fissures opening in the earth. Meanwhile, for many days sweat seeped out of one of the marble statues of Antony near Alba, and, although they tried to wipe it away, it would not stop. While Antony was staying at Patrae, the Temple of Hercules [Antony's mythical ancestor] was destroyed by lightning, while in Athens the statue of Dionysus [the god with whom Antony associated himself most closely] ... was dislodged in a gale and crashed down into the theatre.[120]

How Antony himself responded to these omens is not recorded. Reports do survive, however, of messages sent between him and Octavian, each man goading the other, each calling the other out to battle, as if they were Homeric heroes, or perhaps two suitors fighting to impress a woman:

[Octavian] sent word to Antony challenging him to waste no more time, but to meet him with his forces: Octavian would give him full and unconditional access to the harbours and anchorages and would pull back his army as far as a day's ride from the coast, until such times as Antony had safely landed and set up camp. Antony's reply was just as swaggering, challenging Octavian to single combat, even though Antony was an older man.[121]

Then, even as Antony was thinking up his next red-blooded insult to trade across the Adriatic, news came to Patrae that altered everything. Under the command of his brilliant admiral, Agrippa, Octavian's ships had braved the late-winter seas and captured Methone. Not only were there enemy soldiers in southern Greece, but more worryingly the enemy fleet now had a base from which to harry the great grain convoys that, with the coming of the spring, would soon be lumbering their way from Egypt with supplies so dearly needed by Antony and Cleopatra's men.

Even before the full implications of the capture of Methone had had time to sink in fully, more reports reached Antony. There had been further raids along the coast. Corfu had fallen. Octavian's troop carriers had been spotted in the northern Adriatic, had made shore, had debouched their cargo, 80,000 infantry, 12,000 cavalry. The enemy were heading south in search of battle; their goal the Gulf of Ambracia, where the bulk of Antony's own troops were overwintering.

As if shaking off a sluggish nightmare, Antony, Cleopatra and their generals made haste to join their army, sending urgent messages to those of their forces still strung out along the western coast of Greece to rendezvous at the Gulf of Ambracia, at their camp at Anactorium. Still, news kept coming of Octavian's successes, undermining their mens' morale. When they heard that the town of Toryne had fallen, Cleopatra tried to rally spirits with a stab at barrack-room humour. 'What's so bad about Octavian sitting on Toryne?' she asked 'mockingly', a quip which makes sense only if one knows that as well as being a place-name, 'Toryne' had two other meanings: 'ladle' (or 'dipper') and 'penis'.

Soon, Cleopatra's wit was in even greater demand. Octavian's army had occupied the hill on the northern promontory, now called Mikalitzi, which commanded the entrance to the Gulf, while his ships were patrolling the narrow channel to the sea. Despite all his years of glittering command, Antony had let himself be grossly outmanoeuvred. Somehow, in the shallow, reedy lagoon of Ambracia, he had allowed his fleet and the land troops that protected it to be blockaded.

In the winter months, this would have been a cause for great concern. With the approach of summer it was disastrous. As temperatures rose, the swampy marshland, haunt of pelicans and pygmy eagles, cormorants and bitterns, began to dance with ever denser clouds of mosquitoes. With the mosquitoes came malaria, and with the stagnant water, dysentery – enemies potentially more deadly than any army of Octavian. Antony needed to act quickly.

By the time that he and Cleopatra arrived at the Gulf, however, Octavian was already well dug in. Massive earthworks now surrounded Mikalitzi Hill and ran down to the shoreline and the sea. With all his legions in place, Antony might just attempt to storm them. But his legions were not in place. Many were still marching from their winter quarters, and time was moving on.

As more and more detachments of Antony's army began to arrive at their encampment on the flatlands near Actium on the southern shores of the Gulf, there must have been those who looked towards the temple precinct in their midst and felt a frisson of foreboding. By the water, as if taunting them, there squatted by the lapping waves a shrine to Apollo, the deity Octavian had chosen as his patron. It must have felt as if the gods themselves were trying to infiltrate their lines and turn on them.

To make things worse, each morning Octavian drew his legions up in full battle formation, challenging and ridiculing Antony, hoping to provoke a fight. Still Antony held back, even when he heard that the enemy had intercepted all his transport ships and captured them. At last, however, the time came when he had sufficient troops in place to feel confident enough to attempt to seize the initiative.

From Mikalitzi Hill, where Octavian pitched his camp, the Bay of Actium opens to the South.

He ferried most of his troops across the strait and set up his camp not far from Octavian's; next he sent his cavalry around the bay, to confine the enemy on both sides. It was now Octavian's turn to hunker down.[122]

But there was little Antony could do. Octavian's position was too well fortified. There was stalemate in the Gulf, but even stalemate favoured Octavian. With his fleet bottled in, and his legions tied up desperately trying to find a way to take the hill at Mikalitzi, it was not only Antony's supplies which were running dangerously low. Morale among his men was sinking, too. Gradually, news of further setbacks trickled into Actium: the island of Leucas had fallen to the enemy; then Patrae; and then Corinth. A raid against Octavian's fleet, made under cover of thick sea-fog, seemed for a heart-stopping moment to have met with victory, but not for long. The admiral who led it was defeated and his ships destroyed. Then Antony himself, returning from an expedition north to try to win support there, was intercepted by a squadron of the enemy cavalry and forced to flee back to his camp.

Many years earlier, Pompey, friend of Cleopatra's father Ptolemy the Flautist, had remarked that more men worship the rising than the setting sun. Now, in the Gulf at Actium, it was clear whose sun was sinking. With each new day, another general, another tranche of troops defected to Octavian. Plagued by mistrust, Antony's mood became ever crueller. One Roman senator was even condemned to be physically torn apart.

With such disunity in the high command, even the siege of Mikalitzi Hill appeared to Antony to be untenable. It seemed unsafe to have his men divided between two sites.

> So, under cover of darkness, he withdrew his troops from their entrenchments near the enemy lines, and retreated to the other side of the straits, where his main force was camped. Here provisions began to run out, because [most of] his supply lines were obstructed.[123]

In fact one supply route lay open, and throughout Greece, feelings ran high as cities that until recently had been proclaiming Antony the embodiment of Dionysus were pressed into sending convoys laden with provisions west to Ambracia. Few families were untouched. Plutarch himself records:

> My great-grandfather Nicarchus used to tell how everyone who lived in our town [Chaironeia] was forced to carry a specific amount of wheat on their shoulders down to the sea at Anticyra [on the Gulf of Corinth, a 30km trek from Chaeronea across mountainous terrain], all the while being whipped to make them go more quickly.[124]

In Antony's camp itself the situation was becoming desperate. Disease was rife and, with many more men dying from dysentery and malaria than from contact with the enemy, the smoke from funeral pyres billowed thicker by the day into the scorching skies.

For Cleopatra, the situation must have seemed especially bleak. This, after all, was the second time she had experienced the horrors of an enemy blockade. Eighteen years earlier at Alexandria it had been Caesar's energy and ingenuity that saved the day, his restless refusal to accept the odds stacked up against him, his unshakeable conviction that he could win through. Now, far from Alexandria, at Actium, in the dog days of late summer, Antony's lethargic inability to act could not have appeared more of a contrast.

This, surely, must have been what Cleopatra had feared most when, in Ephesus just eighteen months before, she had insisted that she must accompany the general to Greece. It was, after all, this torpor, this inertia, this gloom of Antony's, which she had had to manage when she landed at the White Village in the wake of his disastrous retreat from Parthia. Then, Cleopatra had been forced to seize the initiative and take Antony back with her to Alexandria. Now, it seemed, with the approach of autumn, she would have to seize the initiative again.

In a final council of war, and facing generals, many of whom now openly despised her for the influence she clearly wielded over Antony, Cleopatra made an impassioned speech. The impasse must be resolved, and the place to do it was at sea. Anything was better than this endless waiting. Ships must be manned. All must be staked on one last daring dice-throw.

Not everyone agreed. Among them was Canidius, commander of the legions. Either because he believed in the wisdom of his advice or simply because by now he could not stomach being dictated to by Cleopatra, he sought to argue otherwise.

> Canidius advised passionately that there would be nothing disgraceful in surrendering the sea to Octavian, who was accomplished in naval warfare thanks to the Sicilian War [against Sextus Pompey]. But it would be deplorable for Antony, a general second to none in his experience of fighting on land, not to take advantage of the strength and equipment of so many legions but rather to scatter his troops among the ships and dissipate his strength. However, it was Cleopatra's opinion – to decide the war at sea – which won out in the end.[125]

In truth, most of those present at the meeting must have known this was the only option. With Octavian's position on Mikalitzi Hill so unassailable, and with their own supply line now so tortuous and their men's morale so low, to stay at Actium was unthinkable. Even if the army managed to retreat, albeit (as in Parthia) pursued and harried constantly, back through the rugged passes of the high massif of central Greece, fording the rivers of the north, crossing somehow onto the shores of Asia, the fleet still needed to break out. And even to break out required a naval battle.

As the council of war broke up, the generals conveyed their orders to their expectant troops. With the army seriously depleted (mostly by disease but in part by defection), there were no longer sufficient oarsmen for the entire fleet. A head-count showed how many ships could still be launched. The rest were stripped of anything useful, hauled up onto the beach beyond the camp and burned. Then those who could fit aboard the fleet, 20,000 heavy infantry, 2,000 archers, bade farewell to the legionaries who must be left behind and filed stony-faced and sullen up the slippery gangplanks and onto the remaining ships. As they were doing so, one centurion, a veteran of many campaigns, is said to have complained to Antony:

> 'General, how can you have no faith in this sword and in these battle scars? How can you pin all your hopes on wretched planks of wood? Leave the Egyptians and Phoenicians to do their fighting at sea, but give us solid earth, where we can make our stand, and either overcome our enemies or die.'

Hatchet-faced, Antony made no reply. All that the once so eloquent orator could do was make a 'gesture of his hand, designed to encourage the man to take heart' and walk on past him. In fact, centurions and men cannot but have observed an anomaly in preparations for a clash at sea. Normally, for the sake of space, both masts and sails were removed from galleys before battle and stored under guard on land. Now, though, they saw them brought on board. They may have seen the war-chests, too, the treasure-boxes and the statues of the gods, all the rich royal accoutrements of Cleopatra's court, being stowed safely in her flagship. Some may have believed the sails were brought on board to help their ships pursue the fleeing enemy; most may have known that, really, they were meant for their own flight.

Now, at last, with all the troops aboard, it was time to face Octavian in battle. With trumpets sounding and orders ringing through the bay, and with adrenalin for battle pumping in their ears, the rowers were about to

An eagle perches between two standards in a galley. Dark brown glass paste intaglio, of the Roman period. Width 1.35 cm. British Museum, 1814,0704.2251

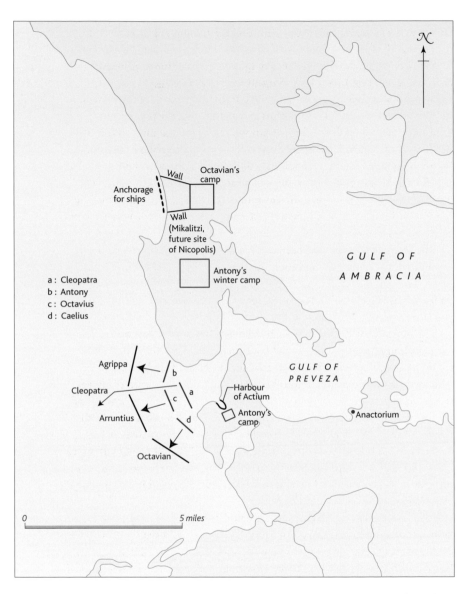

Octavian's camp

Wall

Anchorage for ships

Wall
(Mikalitzi, future site of Nicopolis)

Antony's winter camp

GULF OF AMBRACIA

a : Cleopatra
b : Antony
c : Octavius
d : Caelius

Agrippa

Cleopatra

Arruntius

b

a

c

d

GULF OF PREVEZA

Harbour of Actium

Antony's camp

Anactorium

Octavian

0   5 miles

dip their long oars in the waters of the hateful Gulf, when suddenly and unexpectedly the word came to stand down. A squall was blowing up. A storm was on its way. Reluctantly, the men were taken off the ships, and for three days the army waited in their wind-whipped tents as a gale tore through Ambracia and rollers lashed the promontories and washed across the mudflats by the coast.

At last the winds and rains died down. The storm clouds that had lashed the bay at Actium had rolled away. The sea was calm, the day had come, and onto the looming galleys the army and the hungry, sallow crews once more embarked.

Many of Antony's ships were heavy quinqueremes, bronze-plated at their bows, and fitted with huge rams weighing as much as 300 tons. On many, too, tall wooden towers had been constructed, from the top of which his bowmen could rain down javelins and arrows tipped with fire, while catapults were bolted to the decks from which they could unleash their deadly hail of stones. If the enemy came close, great grappling hooks could be swung down and out to smash into their hulls and render them unusable. But Antony was not relying on ships and men alone. He knew that in the early afternoon the wind would veer round from the north and favour them. With luck and skill, even if they did not win an outright victory, they might at least escape.

The trumpet sounded the command, and slowly the fleet rowed out from the straits by Actium and took up their position, tight-packed, facing out towards the sea, an impenetrable wall of bronze. On the right wing was Antony himself, and behind the crescent of the Roman fleet was Cleopatra and her squadron of Egyptian galleys.

The queen herself was nervous. For some time she, too, had been fretting over troubling omens: swallows had built their nest close to her tent and on her flagship, but other birds had attacked them and killed their chicks. Milk and blood had dripped from beeswax, and (most worrying of all) the statues of herself and Antony as gods, set up on the Acropolis at Athens, had been struck down by thunderbolts and crashed, smashed into pieces in the theatre of Dionysus below. Now, although the day had dawned so fair, a violent rainstorm had begun to lash the waves. High winds were making the seas rough and the ships were rolling dangerously. From her vantage-point on deck, Cleopatra strained in vain to see what was happening beyond the allied ships that towered ahead of her.

On the other side, Octavian was watching, too. His first plan had been to let his enemies slip unharassed out from the bay, and then swoop down and capture Antony and Cleopatra as they tried to flee, but his admiral Agrippa had persuaded him otherwise. They would not catch them, he had said. With the wind in their sails, their quarry would elude them.

In a short while, the rain had stopped. The two sides were lined up. But no one moved. Because they were so undermanned, Antony's heavy ships no longer had the power to ram the enemy. Because Octavian's war-galleys were so much smaller and more vulnerable he did not dare sail closer. So, for a time, both fleets allowed their oars to rest, and waited.

Then suddenly Octavian gave the signal. The two wings of his fleet began to open, stretch and then peel off, the light ships bending round to form a crescent. To Antony the signs were clear. Octavian was aiming to surround

Opposite Map showing the Battle of Actium and surrounding sites (after Cary, M. and Scullard, H. H., *A History of Rome*, Macmillan, London, 1980, p. 296, fig. 24).

The Naval Battle of Actium by Lorenzo A. Castro (active 1672–86), probably inspired by Virgil's *Aeneid* (see pp. 177–8). Oil on canvas, 1672, 108.5 x 158 cm. National Maritime Museum, Greenwich, London.

him. Reluctantly, he bade his trumpeter sound out the order. To the creak of oars and the thump of spray against his ships' bronze-plated hulls, he led his own fleet forward. Like it or not, the battle had begun.

Great cheers and shouts went up from every ship, as captains urged their oarsmen into action. From the decks of Antony's huge galleys, crammed tight with fighting men, massive stones were soon sent screaming through the air from catapults, while archers rained deadly volleys down on the attacking ships. But on Octavian's side were both speed and manoeuvrability. Time and again, his smaller vessels would dart in close below one of Antony's galleys and try to immobilize it. It was as if each side was trying to fight a different type of battle. The accounts of both Plutarch and Dio paint a vivid picture.

Although the fighting was beginning to close in, the ships still did not ram or crush each another – Antony's because their heavy tonnage prevented them from gaining the impetus necessary for a powerful impact; Octavian's because they deliberately avoided a head-on collision against ships which were reinforced with massive metal plates and bronze spikes, and they did not attempt to ram them in their sides, since their beaks would easily have been snapped off when they came into contact with hulls built from huge square timbers bolted together with iron. So the engagement was more like a land battle, or (to be more precise) an assault on a walled city. For three or four of Octavian's ships would surround one of Antony's and the men on board would fight with wicker shields and spears and poles and blazing missiles; Antony's soldiers also fired catapults from wooden towers.[126]

Dio, too, describes it in terms of a land battle.

[Octavian's ships] were like cavalry, one moment charging, the next falling back, since they were prevented from launching an attack or rowing back as they would have liked; [Antony's] on the other hand resembled heavy infantrymen, shielding themselves when the enemy attempted to come to close quarters while at the same time trying to make contact with them. First one side, then the other gained the upper hand, as [Octavian's ships] tore in beneath the banks of oars extending out from [Antony's] ships' sides, shattering the blades, and [Antony's] men with the benefit of taller ships rained down rocks and missiles to sink the enemy.[127]

With battle raging off the two headlands of Actium and Mikalitzi, and the gathering breeze now causing stricken ships to wallow in the choppy waves, few on board the fighting vessels must have been watching Cleopatra's squadron of Egyptian galleys, kept well back and straining at their anchors in the sea-swell. Now, though, observers would have seen an order flashed out from the flagship, sudden action, cross-bars hoisted high on masts, white linen sails unfurled, filled with the wind and bellying. The first ships were nosing out and finding the clear water, arcing south, the breeze behind them, racing now like yachts in a regatta, slicing through the waves and cutting clear to safety.

Then Antony's ship, too, broke ranks. A sudden spurt of speed, the hoisting of a sail, and soon it too was hurtling south, the battle far behind it. Now, in the rest of his bewildered navy, panic and confusion gripped both officers and men alike.

> Some hoisted sails; others threw the towers and anything that they could tear up into the sea, so that, their loads lighter, they could flee more quickly. While they were doing this, Octavian's fleet attacked them: for they had not pursued the escaping ships, since they did not have the proper sails on board, being prepared only for a battle. As a result each one [of Antony's ships] was attacked by many [of Octavian's], both from far off and at close range.

But it was not just those fighting off the coast who had seen Cleopatra's vessels breaking out or Antony's ship following. From his vantage point on Mikalitzi Hill, Octavian had seen them too. Until now, he had hoped that he might capture Cleopatra's treasure chests intact – a tantalizing prize indeed, and one which would help him buy the undying loyalty of his victorious troops – and, for this reason only, he had held back from employing the full force of his arsenal. A treasure ship sunk at sea was, after all, no use to him. Now, though, he was free to unleash utter devastation, to answer fire with fire.

Suddenly, Antony's vessels, with their wooden towers and catapults, found themselves in the eye of a hurricane of flames. Rather than trying to ram them or sheer off their oars, Octavian's fast ships would now row in close,

> pounding them with blazing missiles and hurling torches as if they were javelins; from further off they catapulted jars filled with charcoal and pitch.

The sea was soon an inferno. Antony's fleet, so slow and lumbering, was now a mass of flames. Dio's description is harrowing but worth quoting at length:

> Before the fire ever reached them, some (mainly the oarsmen) were overcome by smoke; but others in the midst of the flames were

roasted as if they were in ovens. Others were incinerated as their
armour grew red-hot. Yet others, either still untouched by the flames
or already half-burned, struggled out of their armour and were
maimed by long-range missiles; or else they dived into the sea and
were drowned; or they were clubbed by the enemies and drowned
that way; or they were torn apart by sea-monsters. In the midst of such
suffering, the only men to die a decent death were those who killed
themselves or one another to prevent them having to endure such
horrors. These men were spared something of the torment, and in the
ships, as on a funeral pyre, their bodies were consumed by the flames.[128]

With the black smoke belching high into the late afternoon sky and
dragging south on the rising wind, its dark stain stretching to where
Antony and Cleopatra's fleeing vessels now had disappeared into the haze,
it was clear to all: Octavian had won a famous victory. Greece was now in
his hands. Before long, Asia must surely follow. And then there would be
only Egypt.

Unless, that is, Antony could somehow rally troops and make a stand.
This was now the only hope to which he and Cleopatra could still cling.
Even this hope, though, seemed too much for Antony. By the time his
galley had caught up with the Egyptian squadron, he had again
sunk into the black lethargy that had so haunted him in the
weeks and months which followed his disastrous Parthian
campaign. On boarding the queen's flagship, he 'did not see
nor was he seen by [Cleopatra]. Instead, he made his way
alone to the front of the ship where he sat down in
silence, his head in his hands'.[129]

Only when a few fast ships from Octavian's
fleet caught up with him and threatened
to do battle did Antony rouse himself. He
ordered his remaining vessels to turn to face
the enemy and managed successfully to
beat them off, but not before Octavian's
captain had rammed one ship, 'spinning
her round like a top', and captured
another 'which contained valuable
dining paraphernalia'. As the
stricken vessel was towed off back
north towards the pall of smoke still
rising over Actium,

Sunk at the Battle of
Actium? This bronze
prow from a boat or
small ship was dredged
up from the outer
bay at Actium. 1st
century BC. Length 47.5
cm. British Museum,
1872,1214.1, donated
by Queen Victoria.

Antony threw himself down in the same position as before and did to move. Three days he spent alone at the prow, perhaps because he was too angry or too shamed to see Cleopatra. Then they docked at Taenarum, where the women of Cleopatra's entourage brought them together to talk, and later persuaded them to dine and sleep together.

Plutarch's account is telling. It was not only Antony who had to be persuaded to speak to Cleopatra. The maid-servants needed to coax Cleopatra, too. Spoken or unspoken, blame and recriminations for the defeat at Actium must never have been far beneath the surface, and that the two found themselves anchored off Taenarum (Cape Matapan) can only have increased their sense of foreboding. For here at the tip of the central southern promontory of the Peloponnese, now called the Mani, in a cave beneath the sea lay what for many centuries men had believed to be one of the entrances to Hades, the underworld, the kingdom of the dead. Its gloomy connotations cannot have been lost on Antony. If anything, they must have further heightened the bleakness of his already sombre mood.

With the arrival of a trickle of transport ships and other vessels that had managed to escape from Actium, the full extent of the disaster became clear. By four in the afternoon, Antony's fleet had surrendered. Three hundred of his ships were captured or destroyed; five thousand of his men had lost their lives. In the immediate aftermath of battle, Antony's men had been bewildered. Many had not even realized that their general had fled. When they did, most of those soldiers who had not embarked onto the ships – whether in the camp at Actium or elsewhere throughout Greece – had gone over to Octavian: nineteen legions and twelve thousand cavalry, 'all undefeated'.

In desperation, Antony summoned his friends and loaded them with gifts, plundering one of his rich transport ships to do so. Then he ordered them to leave, to sail to Corinth and to make their peace with Octavian. Reluctantly (or not) most did.

Plunged into the depths of depression or self-pity, Antony may have allowed himself the luxury of behaving like a man defeated. Cleopatra, on the other hand, could not. She, after all, was still a queen, still ruled a kingdom, still had children whom she hoped might still succeed her, and all was yet to play for. She had managed before to turn circumstances to

Above Celebrations of Victory: silver *denarius* showing Octavian (Augustus) himself and Victory on a prow holding a laurel wreath and palm. Struck in Italy, 29–27 BC. Diam. 1.9 cm. British Museum, R.6168 (see opposite, bottom right, for reverse) and 1901,0407.459.

Opposite A naval trophy set on a prow of a ship, and Octavian standing on a column decorated with ships' rams and anchors. Silver *denarius*, Diam. 1.9 cm. British Museum, R. 6165 and R.6168 (See above, top for obverse).

her best advantage. Now, free from the foetid bay at Actium and once more untrammelled by the constant presence of what she must have seen as Antony's dull, patronizing and misogynistic colleagues, she could again begin to shape her future as she herself saw fit.

The first thing she must do was clear. She must make haste for Alexandria. She must arrive before the news of Antony's defeat. If possible, she must present a show of such great confidence that her subjects in Alexandria, in Egypt and throughout her Ptolemaic Empire would rally to her cause sufficiently for her to seem to hold a position strong enough to let her bargain with Octavian, if that was what it took. As for Antony, he might still have his uses, though what they might be cannot have been immediately apparent. Certainly, Cleopatra could not afford to have his brooding presence by her when she returned to Alexandria.

Racing south, she set Antony ashore west of her capital with a mission to ride to Libya to try to rally troops there. Then, Cleopatra turned her fleet for Alexandria. Already the waters of the sea were stained brown by the rich mud from the Nile; already the scent of Egypt filled the air. Now, as the Pharos lighthouse shimmered, insubstantial, in the distance, already picked out by the rising sun, the royal slaves were busy garlanding the prows with flowers, while up on deck flute-girls began to play, and in her cabin Cleopatra was herself being dressed and made up by her servants.

Soon, on the shore, the cry had gone up that the royal fleet was approaching. Soon, watched so anxiously by many countless thousands, the first of the fleet of proud rich-painted warships entered the royal harbour, its oars like great wings beating rhythmically as it approached the quay. As the ships came closer, it may be that on a given order all the oars in unison rose in salute, held for a long moment high in the air, dripping their wake of molten silver into the shimmering sunlight of the harbour.

This was the signal that the onlookers were waiting for, the sign of triumph, the token clear to all that Cleopatra, Queen Of Kings, Whose Sons Are Kings, The Younger Goddess, Father-Loving, Lover Of Her Fatherland, latest of the line of Ptolemies, had come back to her city, Alexandria, to proclaim that far away at Actium she and her consort, the Roman general Mark Antony, had fought against Octavian. And won.

CHAPTER 10

Dead End

RUTHLESSNESS AND OPTIMISM: like many of her ancestors before her, Cleopatra possessed both qualities in abundance. Now, clinging to the hope that even if she could not turn defeat into victory she could at least salvage the situation sufficiently to allow her to rebuild something of her bargaining base, she set about coldly and mercilessly removing anyone who might oppose her or be seen as a liability. Or those whose estates Cleopatra might herself appropriate. So, in Alexandria and across the Ptolemaic provinces the assassins' blades ran dark with blood. As Dio puts it:

> Once safely ashore, she had many of the most prominent citizens executed on the grounds that they had always hated her and now relished her defeat. By confiscating not only their property but that of religious foundations, too, she raised a considerable amount of money; in fact she did not spare even the holiest of temples in her bid to equip her troops and enlist new allies. She executed Artavasdes, king of Armenia, and sent his head to the king of Media, hoping that this would encourage him to support her cause and Antony's.[130]

Classical sources constantly write like this: as if Antony's and Cleopatra's 'causes' were one and the same, as if their objectives must have been identical. With hindsight, this may well have appeared to be the case, but, in the frenzied weeks and months which followed Actium, to Cleopatra's closest confidantes at least, the situation may not have seemed so simple.

For, to put it brutally, Antony was increasingly becoming a liability. His mission to Libya to secure the support of the army garrisoned there had ended in failure. The commander there had

refused to receive him and had even executed the representatives whom Antony had sent as an advance party, as well as some of his own troops who had expressed their disapproval of such actions.

Pyramus and Thisbe, mythological lovers whose story mirrors that of Antony and Cleopatra, shown on a wall-painting from the House of Octavius Quartio (also known as the House of Loreius Tiburtinus) at Pompeii. 1st century AD.

Plunged even further into his (by now habitual) despondency, Antony had (not for the first time) attempted suicide. It was scarcely the action of a general determined to protect his queen, unless, that is, he believed that, with him dead, Cleopatra would be more free to come to some kind of negotiated settlement with Octavian. Whatever his motivation, Antony was prevented from taking his own life by friends, who conveyed him back with them to Alexandria.

Yet not even Alexandria could revive his spirits. Here, in the city where he had enjoyed so often the most extravagant and lavish parties, where, too, a matter of a few years earlier he had not only ridden through the boulevards in triumph but bestowed on the royal Ptolemaic family all of Rome's eastern empire, Antony now withdrew from company entirely to live the life of a recluse.

> He went to live on the island of Pharos, in a house which he had built on a jetty running into the sea. There he spent his time as a fugitive from humanity, and said that he asked for nothing better than to follow the example of [the 5th century BC misanthrope] Timon . . . like whom he distrusted and hated the whole human race.[131]

According to Strabo, who saw it, Antony's dwelling, the so-called Timonium, was, in fact, 'a royal mansion' built far out on a mole connected to the promontory, on which already rose the temple to Poseidon. Much though Antony may have wished to be alone, he could not bear entirely to eschew the trappings of monarchy. Yet, as Cleopatra gazed out across the great harbour from the high windows of her own royal palace, first towards Antony's Timonium, then to the imposing Caesareum, with its massive porticoes and proud facades, a monument to her mentor, Caesar, she cannot but have drawn comparisons between the two men.

Given the circumstances, what would Caesar have done? Not skulk in solitude like Antony, in a paralysis of depression. Not give in before the final battle had been joined. No, Caesar would have tried his utmost to keep his options open, energetically pursuing every avenue, charismatically wooing allies, making deals, moving heaven and earth to make sure that when conflict came he was in the best position to exploit the situation to his own advantage. So, realizing that her future and the future of her family lay in her own hands, Cleopatra set to work.

Her strategy was two-pronged. Compromise with Octavian was the ideal outcome; but if this failed, flight must remain an option. Again, Dio's account gives something of the flavour of the increasingly tortuous negotiations which the court at Alexandria conducted with Octavian, and the plots (on both sides), which accompanied them:

Hoping either to trick him or even to assassinate him through treachery, they sent envoys to Octavian with peace proposals for him and bribes for his entourage. Meanwhile (unbeknownst to Antony) Cleopatra sent Octavian the golden sceptre, golden crown, and royal throne of Egypt, as if through these symbolic gifts she was offering him her kingdom, and at the same time to ensure that even if Octavian hated Antony, he would at least feel sympathy for her. Octavian considered these gifts to be a good omen and accepted them ... His public response was combative, insisting that only when Cleopatra disbanded her army and stepped down from the throne would he consider what should be done with her. But he communicated with her privately that, if she killed Antony, he would pardon her and let her keep her kingdom undisturbed.[132]

More negotiations followed, with envoys coming to Octavian both from Cleopatra and, in time, from Antony as well. Antony's messages were rambling and maudlin, appealing to old family ties, reminding Octavian of 'sexual encounters and youthful escapades' the two had shared together, offering Antony's suicide in return for Cleopatra's safety. Octavian did not bother to reply. Nor did he reply when he received a further plea, that 'Antony should be allowed to live out the rest of his life as an ordinary citizen in Athens, if it was impossible for him to stay in Egypt'. Indeed, all that such messages from Antony achieved was to confirm that he was broken; Octavian's silence simply served to break him all the more; and, when Antony, in desperation, sent his eldest son Antyllus to Octavian with wagon-loads of gold, Octavian merely sent Antyllus, empty-handed, back to Antony. He kept the money, though.

With Cleopatra, however, Octavian took care to keep open channels of negotiation. More than once he conveyed messages to her 'combining threats with promises'. The threats were to be expected; the promises, however, appeared tantalizingly to offer a way out; they must have seemed engagingly attractive. Given the fraught nature both of the Actium campaign and of its aftermath, even the conditions which Octavian laid

Cleopatra VII wears a triple *uraeus* crown which has three cobras with sun discs on their heads. Hellenistic blue glass intaglio, made in Egypt, 51–30 BC. Height 1.3 cm. British Museum, 1923,0401.676.

down may not have been entirely disagreeable, namely that if she killed or exiled Antony, she herself would be treated fairly.

At some stage in the midst of all this phoney diplomatic war, Octavian sent an envoy of his own to Cleopatra, a freedman chosen for his skills as a negotiator, but possessed of a name which must have caused Octavian to permit himself a rare, if icy, smile. For the freedman was called Thyrsus, and the thyrsus was, of course, the emblem of Dionysus (see p. 87), the god whom Antony believed protected him. The true reasons for Thyrsus' mission are lost to us. No doubt intelligence-gathering formed a major part of it. But it proved useful, too, in planting further doubts in Antony's already suspicious mind.

> Thyrsus was no fool; in fact he was just the right man to conduct
> negotiations between a young commander and a woman who was
> unusually proud of what she perceived as her beauty. As it happened,
> Thyrsus was allowed more time than usual with the queen and was
> clearly held in great respect by her and as a result Antony became
> suspicious. He had Thyrsus arrested and beaten and then sent him
> back to Octavian together with a letter stating that Thyrsus' rude
> and arrogant behaviour had irritated him at a time when, thanks
> to his adversities, he was easily irritated.[133]

How satisfied Octavian must have felt.

Yet, how far to trust Octavian? This must have been the question which most plagued Cleopatra. Without firm assurances, an escape route remained as important as ever, and early in the period of waiting for Octavian to act, Cleopatra began to put in place an elaborate and daring plan which would, she hoped, secure safe passage in the event that she needed to take flight. Where now the Suez canal links the Mediterranean with the Red Sea, Cleopatra, it was said,

> planned to raise her fleet out of the water, haul it overland and launch
> it again in the Red Sea, loaded with vast sums of money and a strong
> army. She would then settle abroad, escaping captivity and war.[134]

In fact, before any such plan could be fully implemented, the local Arab tribes attacked the ships and burnt them. But it did not put a stop to stories in the market-place at Alexandria or within Octavian's high command that Cleopatra was still contemplating an escape. If not to India, to Spain. Or Gaul. Or anywhere she could still rally troops and make a stand. At any time of crisis, the rumour mill becomes unstoppable, the speculation more extravagant, and now was no exception.

Among them was the titillating tale that (despite whatever hopes she may have entertained for her salvation) Cleopatra was preparing for her death, collecting

> every variety of deadly poison, and testing each of them on
> condemned prisoners, to find out which involved least pain. But
> when she discovered that fast-acting poisons caused most suffering,
> while those which involved less pain took effect more slowly, she
> experimented with venomous animals, watching as they were set
> on their victims in front of her. She did this on a daily basis, and
> discovered that only an asp-bite induced lethargy and torpor without
> moaning or convulsions, but rather with only light facial perspiration
> and a dulling of consciousness as victims gradually and gently lost
> their strength and became unresponsive to attempts to rouse or
> waken them, like people who are sleeping soundly.[135]

No one bothered to check that, in fact, the bite of the Egyptian cobra (with which Plutarch's 'asp' can almost certainly be identified), while causing an initial drowsiness, gives rise to vomiting, diarrhoea and respiratory failure, and, as a means of suicide, is unarguably messy and unpleasant. But, then, no one was really interested in the truth of the matter. It all made for a splendid story, exotic, potentially erotic and most certainly blood-thirsty, and that was all that mattered. (In fact, should Cleopatra have had a genuine interest in the properties of poisons, she could without question have discovered all she needed to know from the shelves of Alexandria's great Library or in the notebooks of the Museum specialists. Poison was no stranger to the dynasties who had succeeded Alexander.)

At the same time, other rumours swirled around the city streets. For weeks, they said, Antony had refused to believe what clearly was the truth: that after Actium the loyalty of his now abandoned legions had evaporated, while kings and other allies, who had once supported him and fêted him, had lost no time in abandoning his cause and throwing their hands in with Octavian. Now, though, reality had sunk in. If, up to this point, he had been showing signs of depression, now he was plunged into a paralysis of gloom and total despair.

Perhaps realizing that, for him at least, the game was up, and craving some companionship, he left his Timonium and returned to the palace, where he gave orders for the staging of what he must have seen as one last public celebration: a joint 'coming of age' ceremony for his son Antyllus (by Fulvia) and Caesarion, son of Caesar and Cleopatra. Like the great Donations just over three years earlier (34 BC), the event was held in the

Twin serpents coil on gold spiral bracelets. 1st century BC–1st century AD. Diam. 6.6 cm. British Museum, 1917,0601.2780–2781, bequeathed by Augustus Wollaston Franks.

Gymnasium, and 'involved sumptuous banquets, drinking parties and the bountiful distributions of gifts'.

But now, for Antony at any rate, such festivities assumed a febrile air of fatalistic desperation. In merrier days, he and his friends had formed their *Society of Peerless Bon Viveurs* (see p. 94); now they formed another, that of the *Partners in Death*, whose members, having agreed 'that they would die together, set about spending their remaining days consuming exquisite banquets and enjoying fine wine'. Or so the rumours said. Certainly, Cleopatra made sure that the banquet to celebrate Antony's fifty-third birthday was on a lavish scale (14 January 30 BC). In true Ptolemaic tradition, she used it as an opportunity to distribute extravagant largesse.

With so much speculation merely adding to the growing tension in the streets, there was but one thing of which anyone who endured that brooding Alexandrian winter (31–30 BC) could have been truly certain. Come the spring, Octavian would lead his troops against them. It was only a matter of time.

So, as the days began to lengthen and the temperatures to rise, it came as no surprise to learn that the legions were already on the march. Led from the east through Syria by Octavian himself, and from the west through Libya by Cornelius Gallus, two armies, with the tramp of hob-nailed sandals and the jangling of bridles and the lumbering of all their heavy wagon trains, were already beginning to converge on Alexandria. Yet, even in the midst of such predictability, there was still some room for disbelief. For when, by mid-July, Octavian's men came to the eastern Egyptian border town, Pelusium, rather than put up a fight, its garrison surrendered.

The rumour was that it had done so on Cleopatra's own explicit orders.

Such speculation, though, was academic. More serious and pressing was the stark reality to which the citizens of Alexandria would soon awake. Octavian and his army were at the gates. They were setting up their vast encampment near the Hippodrome, the site of Ptolemy II's by now legendary procession in honour of Dionysus, just to the east of the city. And they were clearly here to stay.

Octavian's presence spurred Antony to action. Already he had tried to stop the advance of Gallus' army from the west. Many of Gallus' troops had once been in Antony's own legions, and Antony could not believe that they were now hostile to him. Surely, he thought, if only they were to see him once again, they would come back to him. So, with a considerable force of infantry and cavalry, he had struck out east, while out to sea ships from the Alexandrian war fleet sailed alongside them, and, at Paraetonium (modern Sollum), he had ridden up, close to the walls, and hailed his erstwhile men. But he was thwarted.

> Gallus gave orders for all his trumpets to blare out at once, and as a result no one could hear anything that was said. Antony then tried unsuccessfully to launch a surprise attack; and later his fleet, too, was defeated. For during the night, Gallus had ordered underwater chains to be stretched across the harbour mouth. In the morning, he seemed to leave the entrance unguarded, condescendingly allowing the enemy to sail in at will; but once they were all inside, he used machinery to raise the chains. Antony's ships were now surrounded on all sides. So Gallus harried them from the land, from the houses and from the sea, setting some on fire and sinking others.[136]

Now Antony had turned and, with his cavalry, had dashed the 250 or so miles (400 km) back to Alexandria. By the Hippodrome he found Octavian's soldiers setting up their camp. Hurriedly Octavian's own cavalrymen saddled up and galloped out to meet him (31 July 30 BC). The two sides clashed, and in the battle which ensued, Antony quite brilliantly rediscovered something of the flair which had so marked him out when he had served with Caesar, routing Octavian's cavalry and sending them in flight back inside the safety of their stockade. Contemptuously, Antony ordered leaflets to be attached to arrows and fired into Octavian's camp, promising a reward of 6,000 sesterces each to every man who should switch sides. Then he wheeled his horse and rode in triumph back into Alexandria.

As he strode proudly into Cleopatra's presence, his tunic streaked with sweat and stained with blood, the queen cannot but have remembered how

Caesar, too, had once come back to her, proud from the fight, when he had torched the fleet in the great harbour and won a crucial victory (see p. 46). Yet, she knew how different things were now. And so did Antony's men. Plutarch records one devastating detail:

> [Antony] strode into the palace, dressed as he was in full armour, kissed Cleopatra, and presented to her one of his soldiers, who had fought with great distinction. As a reward for his bravery, Cleopatra gave the man a golden breastplate and a helmet. The soldier (naturally) accepted them but in the night he deserted to Octavian.[137]

Fuelled by his success, Antony sent a message to Octavian, a challenge, like the challenge he had issued before Actium, to meet in single combat and so decide the outcome, fighting to the death, as if they were Homeric heroes (see p. 140). Just as before, Octavian (predictably) refused. Yet, fresh from his victory that afternoon, Antony was determined to press home what he was convinced was his advantage. Let the next day bring with it battle. He would unleash his full force against Octavian, attacking by both land and sea, and so stake everything on one last throw. It would be death or glory, but it would bring him honour either way.

How Cleopatra viewed all this is not recorded. By now she had her own agenda. If, by some miracle, Antony should win, she would, of course, be gratified. If, on the other hand, events were to take a different course, at least she could be satisfied that the arrangements she had made, both within the palace and with Octavian, might still have the potential to save her. Antony was undoubtedly unstable; and a strange event later that night (whether imagined or real, staged by his enemies to unsettle him further) merely added to his instability.

> They say that in the night, at about midnight, when all the city was quiet and an atmosphere of melancholy and of fear for what the future held hung over it, there suddenly was heard the mingled harmony of many instruments of every kind, and the shouts of a great crowd, the cries of Bacchic revelry, the leaping jump of Satyrs, as if a Dionysiac procession exultantly was leaving the city. It seemed to make its way through the middle of the city and towards the gate, near which the enemy were camped, and here the noise reached a crescendo and then died away. Those who tried to interpret the portent concluded that Dionysus, the god, to whom Antony had likened himself, with whom, indeed, he had most identified, was now deserting him.

Dionysus, Antony would find, was not the only one.

Sunrise saw a frenzy of activity (1 August 30 BC). Orders had already been conveyed from the palace to the fleet and the commanders of both cavalry and infantry. It was to be a coordinated attack, an all-out onslaught against Octavian by land and sea. With his legionaries and auxiliaries stationed on the low hills to the east of Alexandria, Antony watched as the Egyptian fleet, ships which had escaped from Actium eleven months before, and others which had been built over the winter, cast off their hawsers from the quay-side and began to move with regular oar-strokes out across the harbour and towards the open sea.

Here, in familiar waters, would be fought an epic naval battle, where victory for Antony would wreak vengeance for his defeat at Actium. Out, beyond the harbour mouth, Octavian's fleet waited. Now the two lines of ships were drawn up facing one another, motionless. Then, on a signal, and with the thump and splash of oars, Antony's fleet edged forward, picking up speed, heading straight towards the enemy.

But, before they could engage, the unthinkable happened. On every ship of Antony's fleet, the oars in unison rose high and froze, held for a long moment in the air, as the ships glided onwards, in salute. Octavian's fleet responded, oars raised high, and cheers went up from every ship as Antony's vessels, peeling off to either side, slipped in beside Octavian's. 'The two fleets, now united, changed course and made straight for Alexandria'.

Even as Antony was taking in the full horror of the situation, news came to him of his cavalry. They, too, had gone over to the enemy. Only his infantry remained still loyal, and for a brief time they fought bravely. But the odds were stacked against them. They were routed. As he joined his fleeing soldiers, running in panic back inside the gates of Alexandria, Antony was heard to 'shout out angrily that Cleopatra had betrayed him to the very men he was fighting on her behalf'. Indeed, allegations would be later made that Cleopatra had induced the navy to desert, too, part of a deal she had already struck with Octavian.

Certainly, when Antony returned to Alexandria, Cleopatra was nowhere to be seen. Like his navy and his troops, like Dionysus, too, she had abandoned him. In fact, she had retired to her mausoleum, a vast construction, not yet finished, in the heart of the palace parkland, a stone-built edifice as strong as any citadel, and equipped with massive doors, seven metres tall, so heavy that, once in place, they could not be opened. Now, inside and with only her immediate entourage around her, Cleopatra gave the order for the 'doors, strengthened as they were with bolts and bars' to be let down. Entombed she may have been, but she was safe.

And in what must have seemed an oddly powerful bargaining position. For all around her, glinting in the half-light of the torches, was the royal treasure. But not only treasure. As Plutarch records:

Here she collected the most valuable of the royal treasures – gold, silver, emeralds, pearls, ebony, ivory and cinnamon – and in addition great quantities of firewood and pitch.[138]

The threat, which these all preparations implied, was not lost on Octavian, for whom, as for so many Romans, Egypt's riches seemed an answer to his prayers. Indeed, as Dio tells us, Cleopatra had herself spelled out the situation clearly: she had already 'threatened to burn it to the ground with herself inside it, if Octavian refused any of her demands'. Far from fleeing to the mausoleum in panic, as ancient sources would have us believe, Cleopatra's cool withdrawal into this impregnable building, packed with the wealth of Egypt, was part of a cleverly devised plan. On its success hung not only Cleopatra's own life, but the lives of her children and the future status within the Roman Empire of both Alexandria and Egypt. With the stakes so high, there could be no room for mercy, let alone for sentiment.

There was an ancient fable which concerned two lovers, Pyramus and Thisbe. Believing that his beloved Thisbe had been mauled to death by a lion, Pyramus committed suicide by falling on his sword. But Thisbe was alive, and, finding Pyramus' warm corpse, she first wept uncontrollably and then she took the blood-stained sword and she too killed herself. It is a tragic and romantic fable, but a fable nonetheless. From an early stage it cast its mantle over the events which followed Cleopatra's self-entombment to such an extent that the one has become almost indistinguishable from the other. Yet what happened in the frantic hours which followed Antony's infantry defeat outside the walls of Alexandria was the stuff of neither fable nor romance, but politics.

If Cleopatra were to have a future, it could not include Antony. He was a spent force, discarded by his troops, despondent, an impediment to any future settlement. Even if Octavian had not demanded his removal (see p. 157), Cleopatra knew that Antony must go. Yet, she knew, too, how often in the past he had made empty threats of a dramatic suicide, and that for him actually to carry out the deed, no matter how disheartened he might feel, he would need some encouragement.

So, as Plutarch, in a sentence which is almost so casual as to be thrown away, reports, before she entered her mausoleum: 'she sent messengers to Antony with news that she was dead'.[139] Dio expands: 'She hoped that when Antony heard of her death, he would not want to live without her, but would kill himself immediately.'[140] Her hopes were justified. When he heard the news, and thinking he had nothing left to live for, Antony demanded that his slave (whose name, appropriately enough, was Eros) should stab him with his sword. But rather than take his master's life, Eros took his own. With no more options left, Antony drew his own sword and plunged it deep into his stomach. Yet even a clean suicide evaded Antony, and what happened has entered the canon of romanticism.

Somehow, as he lay dying, Antony discovered that Cleopatra was alive. Dio tells us that when he stabbed himself

> there was a great deal of noise. Cleopatra heard it and looked out over the parapet of the mausoleum. The doors to this building were tight shut, and there was no mechanism by which they could be opened, but the upper storey near the roof had still not been completely finished. As a result, people caught sight of her as she looked over the parapet and shouted out so loudly that even Antony heard them. So he knew that Cleopatra was alive. He got to his feet thinking that he still might live. But he had lost so much blood. He knew the end was near. So he begged those who were with him to carry him to the mausoleum and haul him up, using the ropes which had been left hanging there to raise the stones.

Plutarch's account becomes so vivid as to be almost novelistic. Portraying Cleopatra as a second Thisbe, distraught at her lover's suicide, and purporting to use evidence based on eye-witness accounts, he writes of how

> she hauled him up herself, with the help of the only two women, whom she had allowed into the mausoleum with her. According to those who were there, there will never be a more heart-rending sight than Antony, drenched in blood and tortured by the agonies of death, being hauled up, stretching out his arms for Cleopatra as he hung, suspended in the air. It was hard work for a woman, and Cleopatra, her hands clasped tight about the rope, her face strained and grim, could scarcely pull him up, while those below shouted their encouragement and shared her pain.[141]

It is such a vivid image that it cries out to be true. Yet, in the pages which follow this account, Plutarch goes on to describe (in ornate detail) private conversations which took place within the mausoleum, and of which there can have been no record. So, too, does Dio. Unsurprisingly, their accounts are contradictory, for both, essentially, are fiction. As Antony, his body wracked with pain, disappeared inside the darkness of the mausoleum, packed with its glittering treasures, so the objectivity of history went with him. All that remained was the romance, the make-believe of future generations, the manufactured image of a noble Antony dying in his grieving Cleopatra's arms. The reality may well have been very different. Suetonius, for example, tells how Octavian himself ordered Antony to commit suicide and inspected the body afterwards to make sure that he had obeyed, a very different slant on the event, and one (it must be recalled) inspired by the historian's reading of the Roman palace records. Yet, in the end, there was one thing alone that really mattered: Antony was dead. Day one of a new era had begun.

But there was still much which was uncertain; and, in Cleopatra's mind at least, much politicking remained to be done. Locked in her gilded mausoleum, and with the means to destroy the very wealth which she knew Octavian desired, she must have felt relatively secure. She was soon to learn that, even here, she, who had once been praised for her wit and intellect, had been outwitted. For, in the hours which followed Antony's death, Gallus, the general who had defeated Antony at Paraetonium a few days earlier, arrived outside the mausoleum. Through the narrowest of cracks between the outer door and the stone wall, he let it be known that he had come to negotiate.

Their attention now completely focused on Gallus' words, no one in the mausoleum thought to learn what else was going on outside. It was a crucial oversight. For Octavian's men in silence had cleared the area of onlookers, while others brought a ladder, tall enough to reach the open window through which the dying Antony, a few hours earlier, had been hoisted up and in. Then three figures could be seen, three armed men, climbing the ladder stealthily; and, when they reached the top, they quietly dropped inside the mausoleum.

Stories soon circulated about what happened next; how, when the men burst in on her, Cleopatra tried to stab herself; how one of the soldiers flung his arms round her, and snatched the dagger from her hand, and quickly searched her clothes for poison. Again, given the paucity of witnesses, the details may well have been elaborated or even fabricated later. But again, only the headlines really mattered: Cleopatra was under Octavian's control; she had been removed from the mausoleum under armed guard to the palace; and the mausoleum and its contents had been secured.

While all this was going on, Octavian himself had entered Alexandria. The city was on edge. Perhaps the Alexandrians had heard already how Octavian had reacted to the news of Antony's death with tears and expressions of regret. If they had, they would not have been surprised. Such shows were, by now, traditional. Had not Caesar wept when he was shown the head of his arch-rival Pompey, a man to whom he, too, had once been joined by marriage? Yet they might also have heard how, moments later, Octavian produced letters which he and Antony had exchanged and read them aloud in front of his entourage, so that they might compare his own appeasing language with Antony's rude and aggressive replies.

Octavian, in other words, may have been keen to appear compassionate, but he was nonetheless determined to let it be remembered with whom the real blame lay: with Antony.

And with the Alexandrians? There can be little doubt that the citizens were uneasy. At a rally in the gymnasium, the venue Antony had chosen for his Donations four years earlier, they had their first chance to assess their new conqueror.

> When he entered the gymnasium and mounted the tribunal built for him there, the people were paralyzed with fear and prostrated themselves before him. But Octavian ordered them to stand and told them that he absolved them of any blame that might be laid against the people, first in recognition of Alexander, who had founded the city, and second because of the city itself, which he admired for its beauty and its size . . .[142]

But Octavian's clemency extended only so far. Even as the (albeit strained) cheers of the citizens of Alexandria were rising into the August air, squads of soldiers were hunting down Antyllus, Antony's eldest son. They found him whimpering, clinging to a statue of Caesar and begging for mercy. He received none. They dragged him from the statue and beheaded him. Meanwhile, detachments of cavalry were galloping south towards Ethiopia. For they had heard that Cleopatra had already sent her son Caesarion away at the head of a great camel train of gold, his destination: India, with which the Ptolemies had traded for so many centuries. Somewhere they caught up with him and killed him.

In Alexandria itself, Cleopatra remained a prisoner and under constant watch. Among those who attended her was her physician, Olympus, who subsequently exploited his experiences in his memoirs. According to Plutarch (who had access to them), these recorded how Cleopatra fell into an extravagance of mourning for Antony, tearing her breasts in the traditional way while at the same time starving herself.

> In consequence of the grief she had suffered and the pain that she was in (her breasts were inflamed and torn from her beating of them) she became feverish, a welcome excuse for her to refuse food and allow herself to slip away from life unchallenged.[143]

At the same time, however, she was still negotiating with Octavian – not entirely the actions of a woman bent on suicide. Nor was Octavian's response to the news of her deteriorating health that of a man who wished her immediately dead:

> He became suspicious and frightened her with threats about her children, undermining her resistance, as a general undermines a city wall with siege-machinery. So she submitted her body to such care and nourishment as was required.

The sheer weight of contradictions such as these which infest these days has led to a welter of claims and counter-claims, of conspiracy theories and scenarios in which each party tries desperately to outwit the other. Little can be reconstructed with any certainty.

At some stage, Cleopatra seems to have been allowed to give some kind of burial to Antony's body which may have involved embalming it, as a first step towards mummification. According to Plutarch, she

> buried it with her own hands, royally and with great pomp, for which she was given all that she demanded.

So, Antony's wishes were, in the end, observed. He was buried, as in his will he asked to be, in his beloved Alexandria.

At some stage, too, Octavian paid his only recorded visit to any of the usual attractions of the city: the mummified corpse of Alexander the Great, which had lain intact in its sarcophagus for almost three hundred years, the numinous soul of Alexandria.

> He even touched it, as a result of which (or so they say) part of the nose was broken off. But, despite the Alexandrians being very keen to exhibit them, he had no interest in viewing the bodies of the Ptolemies, saying: 'I wanted to see a king, not corpses.' For much the same reason he refused to meet the Apis [bull], remarking 'Gods, yes; cattle, no.'[144]

In his insensitivity to Egypt's beliefs Octavian, the country's conqueror, was far removed from Antony, its ally, or even from Caesar before him. In his vandalism of Alexander's corpse, he demonstrated not only his indifference to the history and glory of the bygone world of Greece, but his sense of his own superiority and of the indisputable power of Rome.

In the end, that power could not embrace Cleopatra. A meeting was said to have taken place between Octavian and the queen, at which Cleopatra offered excuses for her role in the recent war and Octavian, convinced that Cleopatra would 'sail with him to Rome of her own free volition', appeared to offer clemency. In fact, no records of the meeting existed from which any of the ancient sources could form a reasoned view. Their accounts belong as much to fiction as to history.

For his own reasons (and to keep the volatile Alexandrians onside was not the least among them), Octavian struggled to appear to show some sympathy towards the queen. Perhaps he really did wish her to come with him to Rome so that he could parade her in the midst of all his booty through the streets in triumph. But he cannot have been unaware of how the sight of Cleopatra's ill-starred sister Arsinoë had affected the crowds which lined the route through Rome towards the Capitol. He cannot but have feared the backlash of the populace, were they to see the queen of Egypt, charismatic even in defeat, paraded in chains before his chariot. So, even if in Alexandria it seemed best to show compassion, in Rome it might be best to show nothing (or no one) at all.

Cleopatra would not be the last enemy of the state whose death would be less embarrassing than her continued living. With well-placed rumours circulating wildly about her grief for Antony, her mental instability, her passionate desire (like Thisbe at the death of Pyramus) to die, it can have come as no surprise to anyone when, a full ten days after the suicide of Antony, news of Cleopatra's death was finally released. Yet, despite the fact that the queen had been under constant military watch or the presence of so many eminent physicians in the court at Alexandria, there were as many stories about how Cleopatra died as there were people to tell them.

According to Plutarch, Cleopatra bathed and then lay down in Antony's tomb to enjoy a sumptuous meal. A basket of figs was brought in to her; a letter to Octavian was carried out; the doors were closed; now in the tomb were only Cleopatra and two waiting women. The letter turned out to be a suicide note, and when the doors of the tomb were opened Cleopatra was already dead. Only one of the women was still living. Her last words were that 'for a princess descended from so many kings, it had been done properly and well'. Yet even Plutarch admits that he is baffled about what really happened:

> It is said that, in accordance with Cleopatra's instructions, an asp was brought in to her, hidden under the leaves in a basket of figs, so that the snake might bite her without her knowing. But when she took out some of the figs, she saw it, and said, 'So it really was there!' Then she bared her arm and she held it out to be bitten. But other people say that the asp was carefully enclosed in a water jar and that, as Cleopatra was provoking it with a golden spindle, it sprang up and

locked itself on her arm. No one really knows the truth: there is even another version that she carried poison with her in a hollow hair-pin which she kept hidden in her hair. What we do know is that no rash or any other sign of poison showed on her body. In fact, the asp was never seen inside, though some people claimed to have seen traces of its trail beside the sea, next to the building, where there were windows. Some people even say that two punctures, small and faint, were found on Cleopatra's arm . . .[145]

As Plutarch is at such pains to point out, there is so much hearsay and so much which does not add up: the absence of a guard within the chamber; the poisoned phial (presumably overlooked in body searches); the lack of symptoms; the identity of the asp which somehow managed to kill three women and then evaporate into thin air; the report of Cleopatra's last words, when none who might have heard them had survived to record them. As Plutarch himself says, 'no one really knows the truth'. Except perhaps Octavian.

He made an ostentatious show of trying to revive her, even (so it was said) 'employing snake-charmers to suck the poison from the wound'. But, of course, it was no use. Claiming that

> he admired her noble spirit, he gave orders that Cleopatra's body should be buried with royal pomp and splendour beside that of Antony, and that her serving-women too should receive honourable funerals.

Within two days of Cleopatra's death, Octavian left Alexandria on a vessel bound for Syria (12 August 30 BC), where he would overwinter before returning in triumph to Rome (see below). As Prefect of Egypt, he appointed Cornelius Gallus, who had defeated Antony and then tricked Cleopatra. But like generations of Romans before him, Octavian was wary. He knew that the wealth of Egypt still held the potential to finance insurrection, so,

> because of the large numbers of people both in the cities and in the country, people whose nature was both impressionable and quick to change, because, too, of the grain supply and the great wealth, he could not possibly entrust the territory to a senator. In fact, he would not even let one to live there, unless he gave personal permission to the individual by name.[146]

In Alexandria itself, Octavian disbanded the city council, 'presumably since he thought them addicted to revolution', while along the banks of the Nile gleaming statues of the conquering Roman were erected, reminders to the teeming people of its fertile land, of their new overlord. And this, as Dio the historian concludes, 'was how Egypt was enslaved'.

The Death of Cleopatra by Jean-André Rixens (1846–1925). 1874, oil on canvas, 200 x 290 cm. Musée des Augustins, Toulouse.

Right Now the empire's undisputed ruler, Octavian becomes Augustus. Bronze head (known as the Meroe Head), made in Egypt, *c*.27–25 BC, and found at Meroe in Sudan. Height 43 cm. British Museum, 1911,0901.1, donated by the Sudan Excavation Committee with a contribution from The Art Fund.

Opposite 'Aegypto Capta' ('Egypt Captured'): Egypt is shown as a crocodile. Silver *denarius* of Octavian (Augustus), struck in Italy, 28 BC. Diam. 1.9 cm. British Museum, 1866,1201.4189.

Epilogue

'The evil that men do lives after them; the good is oft interred with their bones.'[147] Such was the case with Cleopatra. Octavian and his lackeys in the Roman Senate made swift to see that it was so. Even before the conquering army returned to the empire's capital in triumph, the gloating voices of the victors could be heard. Yet already as they pedalled the official (if improbable) version of Cleopatra's death – that, bitten by asps she had poisoned herself – many found it impossible to resist a certain admiration for what they saw as the queen's nobility.

In the days and weeks after news of Cleopatra's death arrived in Rome, the poet Horace may have been among the first to respond. His Ode (which famously begins *nunc est bibendum*) is an uneasy mixture of jubilation, xenophobia and compassion:

> Now is the time to drink, now, free at last, to pound the ground with feet. Now is the time, like dancing priests of Mars, to decorate the couches of the gods – and feast, friends!

> Just recently it would have been gross sacrilege to fetch the best Caecuban wine up from the dusty cellar, while the mad Queen was plotting ruin for our Capitol, destruction for our empire,

> with her grubby pack of diseased eunuch perverts, uncontrolled in her greed and drunk with sweet fortune!

> But scarcely one ship sailed safe from the flames. No, Caesar sobered up her addled mind, drugged with the wine of Alexandria, returning it to its proper state of fear, when he chased her from Italy

> urging on his oarsmen, fast – like a hawk which swoops on a trembling dove, or a huntsman high in the snowy plains of Thessaly pursuing a hare – to chain that fatal monster. Yet she preferred a nobler death, and (so unlike

a woman) found no fear in the sword; nor did she make for far-off shores with her fast fleet.

No, boldly, calmly, she surveyed her prostrate palace, bravely grasped the hissing asps, that her whole body might drink deep of the black poison

and, in the face of death now fiercer than before, she perished. Clearly a woman, proud as she, would not willingly be led, a private citizen, degraded through the streets of Rome in triumph.[148]

Already, an 'official' picture of Cleopatra is beginning to emerge: 'mad, uncontrolled and drunk', plotting the destruction of Rome itself, brazenly preferring suicide to flight. And no mention at all of Antony.

At the same time, the Senate had scurried to pass as many resolutions as they could in honour of their new master's victory at Actium.

They voted him a triumph for his victory over Cleopatra, and approved the construction of an arch decorated with trophies in his honour at Brundisium, with another in the Roman Forum. They furthermore decreed that the base of the statue of the divine Julius Caesar should be embellished with the rams of warships captured in battle, that a five-yearly festival should be held in Octavian's honour, that the day both of his birthday and of the announcement of the victory should be declared holy, and that, on his entry to Rome, the Vestal Virgins, the Senate and the people, together with all their wives and children, should come out to meet him.[149]

In such an atmosphere of frenzied idolizing of Octavian, the propaganda against Cleopatra, both as a person and as an enemy queen, was ramped up further. Caesar's triumph for his victory in the Alexandrian War may have

The gods commemorate Actium: Flattened image of the Guilford Puteal, a cylindrical marble monument, later turned into a well-head, decorated with Apollo, Artemis, Hera and other deities and nymphs. Erected in Corinth as part of a monument to Actium. 31–1 BC. Height 50 cm; diam. 160 cm. British Museum, 2003,0507 1

needed to be circumspect – then Egypt remained an ally, and he needed to tread carefully (see pp. 61–2). Not so Octavian's (AD 29). With his victory over Antony and Cleopatra, Octavian had subjugated once and for all the Ptolemaic Empire. No need for him to worry about offending sensibilities. He could unleash the full triumphal panoply.

He did. For two raucous days his army pounded the streets of Rome, first celebrating his fleet's victory at Actium, then glorifying his defeat of Egypt.

> Even the other processions took on a magnificent appearance thanks to the spoils from Egypt. In fact, there were so many of them that they could furnish all the processions. But the Egyptian triumph was the most spectacular. Amidst everything else which was carried through the streets was a model of Cleopatra lying dead on her couch. So, in a way, she too was part of the spectacle, alongside the other captives, indeed alongside her children Alexander, named Helios, and Cleopatra, named Selene. Behind them all came Octavian, riding in his chariot and behaving exactly as tradition demanded . . .[150]

In fact, it was not a dead Cleopatra, but the dying one who was carried aloft in effigy. The poet Propertius, himself an eyewitness to the triumph and addressing the dead queen, wrote of how he saw 'your arms bitten by the sacred asps, and your limbs dragging sleep in by a hidden path.'[151] Fired by the passion of the procession, Propertius gives vent to the wrath of Roman popular opinion, no doubt expressed with full-throated vitriol by the crowds packing the streets to the Capitol:

> Surely that whore-queen of incestuous Canopus, scorched as she was by the blood of Philip, dared to oppose our Jupiter with barking Anubis, and to force our River Tiber to endure the threats of her Nile, to drive out our Roman trumpet with the rattle of the sistrum, to pursue our warships with her punted barge, to spread her hideous

mosquito nets over our Tarpeian Rock, and sit in judgement on our Capitol surrounded by Marius' statues and weapons.[152]

Meanwhile, Octavian and his advisors, recognizing that victory in battle was more noble than conquest won through the ambiguous death of a charismatic queen, began to invest Actium with ever greater significance.

> To mark its date (2 September 31 BC) [Octavian] dedicated to Apollo of Actium a trireme, a quadrireme and one of each of the other types of warship up to a decereme, all ships captured in the battle, and he built another bigger temple there. In addition, he inaugurated athletic games and a musical contest, along with horse-racing, too, a sacred festival to be held every four years ... and he named it the Actia.[153]

Meanwhile on the northern of the two promontories which all but enclose the vastness of the Gulf of Ambracia, Octavian founded a new city,

> on the site of his camp; he achieved this by gathering in some of the nearby inhabitants and removing others, he gave it the name 'Nicopolis' [City of Victory]. On the site of his own tent, he constructed a plinth of square stones, and he embellished it with the rams of captured ships. On it he built a shrine for Apollo, open to the sky.

Actium became the focus, too, of the court poet Virgil's description of Octavian's rise to power in the great Roman epic, the *Aeneid*. Written over ten years and unfinished at its author's death (19 BC), the *Aeneid* was a hymn to a new era, where the horrors of almost a century of civil wars were followed by an age of peace and prosperity in an empire ruled by a firm yet beneficent first citizen.

Early in the period of the *Aeneid*'s composition (27 BC), the Senate had voted Octavian two titles. The first, *Princeps*, recognized him as its leader; the second, *Augustus* ('Venerable'; 'Hallowed'; 'Distinguished'), went further. It seemed to invest its bearer with almost godlike qualities: Olympian, timeless and unassailable. It was said to have been suggested by Lucius Plancus, who had once painted himself blue and wriggled naked across the floor at one of Antony and Cleopatra's parties (see p. 131), a curious yet, in the greater scheme of things, irrelevant accident of fate. Such seemed the power and significance of the new epithet that from the moment of its being conferred, its holder was known only as Augustus Caesar. Even the month in which Octavian had won supreme control of the Roman Empire was renamed to commemorate his new title. To this day, the date on which Mark Antony died is known as the first of August.

Yet it was never truly politic for Augustus to vaunt his defeat of a fellow citizen. In the *Aeneid*, as elsewhere, it is Cleopatra who is singled out as the real enemy. Two thirds of the way through the epic poem, Virgil describes a magic shield given to the mythical hero Aeneas. On it, the blacksmith god Vulcan has hammered scenes from what in the context of the poem is Rome's glorious future. Chief among these is a depiction of the battle of Actium. The passage is lengthy but instructive, for it epitomizes the official Augustan view of history:

> The sea was shown there, broad, tempestuous, made in gold; yet still it shone blue, flecked with white foam; and round it, in a circle, silver dolphins leapt, lashing the water with their tails, carving the waves. In the middle, you could see two bronze fleets, Actium, the ships drawn up in ferment round Cape Leucas; and the sea was flashing gold. Here was Augustus Caesar, standing tall on his ship's prow, leading his Italians to battle, the Senate and the People, the gods of the household and the gods of state. And from his helmet twin flames shot up high in joy, while on his crest appeared his father's star. Elsewhere, Agrippa, conspicuous, loved by the winds and the gods, leads out his squadron – on his forehead the naval crown glitters, bristling with beaks, the proud badge of war. There, on the other side, Antony, with his barbaric wealth and his disparate troops, victor over

all the East and the Indian Sea. With him comes Egypt, the strength
of the East and of farthestmost Bactria; and behind him (how
impious!) his Egyptian wife. The fleets rush together, the whole sea
is foaming and churning as oars beat and rams, three-toothed, close
for the fight. They seek the open sea. It looks as if islands, uprooted,
are rushing together or high mountains clashing with mountains,
such is the size of the galleys on one side attacking the turreted ships
of the other. Blazing pitch and iron-tipped weapons tear through
the sky, and the sea's face turns red with new slaughter. At the heart
of battle, the Queen rallies her squadron with Egyptian sistrum (she
still cannot see the twin snakes coil behind her). Barking Anubis and
all of those monstrous misshapen deities are fighting with Neptune,
Minerva and Venus. Where the fighting is fiercest, Mars, made in iron,
is wreaking his havoc, and above, in the sky, are grim Furies. And
Discord, exultant, swoops down, her dress ripped, and Bellona, too,
with a whip dripping blood. Above, as he sees this, Apollo of Actium
draws back his bow, and in terror all Egypt and India, all of Arabia,
all the Sabaeans turn tail in flight. You could see her, the Queen,
calling the winds to fill her sails, already paying out the ropes, ready
to flee. In the midst of the slaughter, Vulcan had shown her pallid
with death to come, borne on the waves by the Westerly wind – and
near her the Nile, his great frame already in mourning, throwing
wide the folds of his watery robes, calling the conquered to come to
his bosom, his blue river haven. But, in triumph Caesar, has entered
Rome . . .[154]

Actium has become an existential struggle between west and east,
between the 'civilized' gods of Rome and the 'barbaric' gods of Egypt.
Truth, the first casualty of war, has been sacrificed to propaganda.

Yet even Virgil could not completely blacken Cleopatra's memory.
Just as Horace's *Ode* had contained a schizophrenic mixture of loathing
and compassion (see pp. 173–4), so, in the *Aeneid*, Virgil can be seen as
painting a much softer, much more sympathetic portrait of the queen. For
Cleopatra is undoubtedly the model for the Carthaginian queen Dido,
who detains the wandering Aeneas on his quest for Italy and makes him
almost forget his divine mission. Even the lights suspended from the roof
and the goblets used at their first meeting remind the reader of the banquet
Cleopatra gave for Antony at Antioch (see p. 91):

burning lamps hang from a panelled golden ceiling, and flaming torches drive away the night. Then the Queen asked for a wine-cup, heavy with jewels and rich with gold, and she filled it up with wine . . .[155]

And when Dido kills herself, throwing herself onto a blazing pyre out of love for the departed Aeneas, it is disturbingly uncertain which character it is with whom the reader is meant to sympathize.

In the real world, even during the reign of Augustus, there was still one last remaining Cleopatra who would be an African queen. For, having been paraded through the streets in triumph, the children of the royal Egyptian court, Cleopatra Selene and her brother Alexander Helios were taken to the house of Octavia, who had once been their father Antony's wife, to be looked after there. When she was old enough, Augustus furnished a rich dowry and arranged a marriage for Cleopatra Selene to King Juba of Mauretania, who himself had once walked in chains before a victor's chariot in Julius Caesar's triumph over Africa (see p. 62).

Together Juba and Cleopatra Selene would have a son, whom they would name from her forefathers, Ptolemy, and he, in turn, would rule until, the last of a long dynasty, he was deposed and killed by the Roman emperor Caligula (r. 37–41 AD), himself the great-grandson of Antony and Octavia.

But it was the death of the last surviving child of Antony and Cleopatra which seemed to be most suffused with significance (5 BC?). For the passing of Cleopatra Selene, whose name meant 'the Moon', was accompanied by a lunar eclipse. The symbolism was not lost on anyone. Crinagoras, a poet originally from Miletus, wrote her epitaph, though it could well serve, too, as a memorial for the lost world she had left behind so many years before at Alexandria:

> Rising as the sun sank, the Moon herself grew dark,
> And in the black night veiled her grief,
> For she had seen her namesake, beautiful Selene,
> Go down to Hades, robbed of breath.
> Once she had shared with her the beauty of her light,
> And now she lent her darkness to her death.[156]

Notes

1. The description of Alexandria in this chapter is based on ancient sources including Caesar's *Alexandrine War* and Strabo's *Geography* (17) as well as on modern archaeology (see e.g. Empereur).
2. Galen, xvii.a, p.607
3. The description of the procession (hotly contested by modern academics) comes from Athenaeus, *Deipnosophistae*, 5.197f.
4. Athenaeus, *Deipnosophistae*, 5.204f
5. This and the following references come from Herodotus, *Histories*, Book 2.
6. Strabo, *Geography*, 17.17
7. This is the Rosetta Stone, now in the British Museum
8. Strabo, *Geography*, XVII. 1. 11
9. Plutarch, *Life of Antony*, XXVII
10. Plutarch, *Life of Pompey*, 79
11. Caesar, *Civil War*, III.106
12. Plutarch, *Life of Pompey*, 80
13. Cleopatra's charms: Cassius Dio, *History of Rome*, XLII.34; Caesar's reputation: Suetonius, *Life of Julius Caesar*, 51
14. The story is contained in Plutarch, *Life of Caesar*, 49 and Cassius Dio, *History of Rome*, XLII.34
15. Caesar, *Civil War*, 110
16. Plutarch, *Life of Caesar*, 49; Seneca, *On the Tranquility of the Mind*, 9.4; Aulus Gellius, *Attic Nights*, 7.17
17. Caesar, *Alexandrian War*, 1
18. Caesar, *Civil War*, 3.112
19. Caesar as executioner: *Civil Wars* 3.112; Caesar's claim: Plutarch, *Life of Caesar*, 49.4–5
20. Caesar, *Alexandrian War*, 2
21. Caesar, *Alexandrian War*, 3
22. Caesar, *Alexandrian War*, 6–7
23. Caesar, *Alexandrian War*, 9
24. Caesar, *Alexandrian War*, 11
25. Caesar, *Alexandrian War*, 18
26. Plutarch, *Caesar*, 49.7-8. The story is repeated in Cassius Dio, *History of Rome*, 42.40
27. Caesar, *Alexandrian War*, 24
28. Caesar, *Alexandrian War*, 31
29. Appian, *The Civil Wars*, 2.13.90
30. Caesar, *Alexandrian War*, 33
31. Suetonius, *Caesar*, 52.1
32. Cassius Dio, *History of Rome*, 43.21.1
33. Pothinus: Appian, *Civil Wars*, 2.101; Ganymedes: scholiast on Lucan *Civil War*, 10,521
34. Cassius Dio, *History of Rome*, 43.19.3
35. Appian, *Civil Wars*, 2.101
36. Lampreys: Pliny, *Natural History*, 9.171; wine: ibid., 14.97
37. Suetonius, *Caesar*, 39
38. Cassius Dio, *History of Rome*, 42, 22,1-3
39. Appian, *Civil Wars*, 2.102; Cassius Dio, *History of Rome*, 51.22.3
40. Suetonius, *Caesar*, 44
41. Philo, *On the Embassy to Gaius*, 151
42. See H. Volkmann, *Cleopatra: A Study in Politics and Propaganda*, Elek, London, 1958, p.77. Sadly we must rely exclusively on this description for our knowledge of the birth temple. In the 19th century its materials were recycled to build a sugar factory.
43. Cicero, *Letters to Atticus*, 15.15.2 In this letter, he seems to suggest that Cleopatra promised him a gift of some books, which were never forthcoming.
44. Making Cleopatra his wife: Nicolaos of Damascus, *Life of Augustus*, 28; proposed law: Suetonius, *Caesar*, 52.3
45. Effigy in hippodrome: Suetonius, *Caesar*, 76; ribbons on statue: ibid., 75; verses: ibid., 80
46. Suetonius, *Caesar*, 79
47. Suetonius, *Caesar*, 82
48. Plutarch, *Life of Caesar*, 6.12–13
49. Cicero, *Letters to Atticus*, 14.20.2
50. May 17: Cicero, *Letters to Atticus*, 15.1.5; May 24: ibid., 15.4.4
51. Plutarch, *Life of Publicola*, 9.6; Dionysius of Halicarnassus, *Roman Antiquities*, 5.17.2
52. Plutarch, *Brutus*, 20
53. Suetonius, *Julius Caesar*, 84
54. This, and the next two extracts, come from Appian, *Civil Wars*, 2.146–47
55. Plutarch, *Brutus*, 20
56. Suetonius, *Julius Caesar*, 84
57. In 2012 this is worth approximately £3,000,000 or $5,000,000.
58. This, and the next four extracts, come from Plutarch, *Life of Antony*, 2–9
59. The sambuca was a type of four-stringed lyre, most often played by girls. Athenaeus, *Banquet of the Sophists*, 129a describes the appearance of some sambuca-players at a party he once attended: 'I thought they were totally naked, but some of my fellow guests assured me they were in fact wearing *something*'.
60. Appian, *Civil Wars*, 4.128
61. Plutarch, *Life of Antony*, 24
62. This, and the next three extracts, come from Plutarch, *Life of Antony*, 25–26
63. Plutarch, *Life of Antony*, 26
64. Plutarch, *Life of Antony*, 25
65. This and the following descriptions come from Athenaeus, *Banquet of the Sophists*, 147–48
66. Plutarch, *Life of Antony*, 27
67. Appian, *Civil Wars*, 5.8
68. Plutarch, *Life of Antony*, 28
69. Appian, *Civil Wars*, 5.8
70. Appian, *Civil Wars*, 5.8
71. Plutarch, *Life of Antony*, 28
72. Plutarch, *Life of Antony*, 29
73. Plutarch, *Life of Antony*, 29
74. British readers might be tempted to think of Antony's group of friends as a proto-Bullingdon Club.
75. Plutarch, *Life of Antony*, 28
76. Plutarch, *Life of Antony*, 28
77. Pliny, *Natural History*, 33.14
78. Plutarch, *Life of Antony*, 29
79. Plutarch, *Life of Antony*, 10
80. Cassius Dio, *History of Rome*, 48.5.3
81. Cassius Dio, *History of Rome*, 48.27.1
82. Athenaeus, *Banquet of the Sophists*, 148b, quoting Socrates of Rhodes
83. Cassius Dio, *History of Rome*, 48.30
84. Plutarch, *Life of Antony*, 33
85. Appian, *Civil Wars*, 5.76
86. Plutarch, *Life of Antony*, 33
87. Cassius Dio, *History of Rome*, 48.39.2. The glosses in square brackets are the present authors' own.
88. Plutarch, *Life of Antony*, 36
89. Plutarch, *Life of Antony*, 36
90. Plutarch, ibid.
91. This and the next extract come from Suetonius, *Life of Augustus*, 70
92. Suetonius, *Life of Augustus*, 70
93. Anon., *Homeric Hymn*, 31
94. This and the quotation in the next paragraph come from Plutarch, *Life of Antony*, 37

95 This and the next two passages come from Plutarch, *Life of Antony*, 39–40
96 Plutarch, *Life of Antony*, 40
97 Cassius Dio, *History of Rome*, 49.28.3f.
98 Cassius Dio, *History of Rome*, 49.30.1f.
99 Plutarch, *Life of Antony*, 45
100 Plutarch, *Life of Antony*, 49
101 This and the next extract comes from Plutarch, *Life of Antony*, 43
102 Plutarch, *Life of Antony*, 37
103 Plutarch, *Life of Antony*, 51
104 Cassius Dio, *History of Rome*, 49.31.4
105 This and the next extract comes from Plutarch, *Life of Antony*, 53
106 Appian, *Civil Wars*, 5.135
107 Plutarch, *Life of Antony*, 54
108 Velleius Paterculus, 2.82
109 Plutarch, *Life of Antony*, 54
110 So Cassius Dio, *History of Rome*, 49.40.3, calls it.
111 Suetonius, *Augustus*, 69
112 Pliny, *Natural History*, 9.119–121
113 Velleius Paterculus, 2.83.3
114 This and the next extract comes from Cassius Dio, *History of Rome*, 50.5
115 Cassius Dio, *History of Rome*, 50.5.4
116 This and the next two extracts come from Plutarch, *Life of Antony*, 56–7
117 Plutarch, *Life of Antony*, 58
118 Plutarch, *Life of Antony*, 59
119 Cassius Dio, *History of Rome*, 50.8.1
120 Plutarch, *Life of Antony*, 60
121 This, and Cleopatra's quip about Toryne, come from Plutarch, *Life of Antony*, 62
122 This, and the next extract, come from Cassius Dio, *History of Rome*, 50.13–14
123 Cassius Dio, *History of Rome*, 50.14.2
124 Plutarch, *Life of Antony*, 68
125 This, and the next extract, come from Plutarch, *Life of Antony*, 63–64
126 Plutarch, *Life of Antony*, 66
127 This, and the next three extracts, come from Cassius Dio, *History of Rome*, 50.32–35
128 Cassius Dio, *History of Rome*, 50.34
129 This and the next quotation come from Plutarch, *Life of Antony*, 67–68
130 This and the next extract come from Cassius Dio, *History of Rome*, 51.5
131 Plutarch, *Life of Antony*, 69
132 Cassius Dio, *History of Rome*, 51.6
133 Plutarch, *Life of Antony*, 73
134 Plutarch, *Life of Antony*, 69
135 Plutarch, *Life of Antony*, 71
136 Cassius Dio, *History of Rome*, 51.9
137 This and the next extract come from Plutarch, *Life of Antony*, 74–75
138 Plutarch, *Life of Antony*, 74
139 Plutarch, *Life of Antony*, 76
140 This and the next extract come from Cassius Dio, *History of Rome*, 51.10
141 Plutarch, *Life of Antony*, 77
142 Plutarch, *Life of Antony*, 80
143 This and the next two extracts come from Plutarch, *Life of Antony*, 82
144 Cassius Dio, *History of Rome*, 51.16
145 This and the next extract come from Plutarch, *Life of Antony*, 87
146 This and the quotations in the next paragraph come from Cassius Dio, *History of Rome*, 51.17
147 Shakespeare, *Julius Caesar*, Act III Scene 2
148 Horace, *Odes*, 1.37
149 Cassius Dio, *History of Rome*, 51.19. Almost a century later (AD 60) the British queen Boudica was said to have committed suicide for the same reason (*see* Moorhead, S. and Stuttard, D., *The Romans Who Shaped Britain*, Thames and Hudson, London, 2012, p. 82)
150 Cassius Dio, *History of Rome*, 51.21
151 This and the next quotation come from Propertius, *The Elegies*, 3.11
152 Propertius, *The Elegies*, 3.11
153 This and the next extract come from Cassius Dio, *History of Rome*, 51.1
154 Virgil, *Aeneid*, 8.671ff.
155 Virgil, *Aeneid*, 1.726–7
156 Crinagoras, XVIII

Further Reading

There have been many books written about Antony and Cleopatra. The following are a selection:

Bradford, E., *Cleopatra*, Penguin, 1971
Grant, M., *Cleopatra*, Weidenfeld and Nicolson, 1972
Goldsworthy, A., *Antony and Cleopatra*, Weidenfeld and Nicolson, 2010
Jones, P. J., *Cleopatra: A Sourcebook*, University of Oklahoma Press, 2006
Schiff, S., *Cleopatra: A Life*, Virgin Books, 2010
Southern, P., *Cleopatra*, Tempus, 1999
Southern, P., *Mark Antony: A Life*, Amberley, 2010
Walker, S. and Higgs, P., *Cleopatra of Egypt*, British Museum Press, 2001

Excavation of Ptolemaic and Roman Alexandria continues apace and new discoveries are made. The following books are recommended:

Empereur, J-Y, *Alexandria Rediscovered*, British Museum Press, 1998
Hawass, Z. and Goddio, F., *Cleopatra: The Search for the Last Queen of Egypt*, National Geographic Society, 2010
Macleod, R. (ed), *The Library of Alexandria*, The American University in Cairo Press, 2000
William la Riche, *Alexandria, The Sunken City*, Weidenfeld and Nicolson, 1997

Finally, translations of most of the classical authors quoted or cited are available from Penguin Books or (increasingly) on the internet.

Index

Picture credits

Every effort has been made to trace the copyright holders of the images reproduced in this book. All British Museum photographs are © The Trustees of the British Museum.

Maps on pp. 6–7, 18, 36 and 146 by David Hoxley, Technical Map Services

Page
12   © JP Golvin
14   © Ross Thomas
42   Alexandria Graeco-Roman Museum; © Roberta Tomber
44   © Jeffrey Spencer
55   © Richard Parkinson
56   © Richard Parkinson
58   © Sam Moorhead
64   © Sam Moorhead
65   Staatliche Museen zu Berlin; © akg-images

72   © Egyptian Museum, Cairo
77   The National Trust, Kingston Lacy, The Bankes Collection; © NTPL/Paul Mulcahy
83   © Richard Parkinson
95.   © Sam Moorhead
120   © David Stuttard
129   The Metropolitan Museum of Art, New York; © Photo Scala, Florence, 2011
135   © Sam Moorhead
142   © Dario Calomino
148   © National Maritime Museum, Greenwich, London
154   © Paul Roberts
171   Musée des Augustins, Toulouse, France; © Photo: akg-images / Erich Lessing
176   © Dario Calomino

Acknowledgements

Like the denizens of the ancient Museum and Library at Alexandria, able to draw on the help of so many experts in so many fields, we have greatly valued the guidance and suggestions of friends and colleagues. At the British Museum, Richard Abdy, Ian Jenkins and Richard Parkinson all gave invaluable advice, while Peter Higgs generously read and commented on the draft text. Any errors that have since appeared are entirely our own. Colleagues have been bountiful, too, in the provision of photographs to enhance the text, and our thanks go to Dario Calomino, Stephen Dodd, Richard Parkinson, Paul Roberts, Jeffrey Spencer, Ross Thomas, Roberta Tomber and Michael Winckless as well as to the British Museum's Department of Photography and Imagery for furnishing such an opulence of images.

At the British Museum Press, we are indebted to Rosemary Bradley, Director of Publishing, and Naomi Waters, Commissioning Manager, for supporting the commissioning of the book; to Charlotte Cade for producing it; to Axelle Russo-Heath for picture research; to David Hoxley for his clear cartography and to Bobby Birchall for such stunningly beautiful design. Especial thanks are due, however, to our incomparable editrix, Emma Poulter, who, with the wiles, wit and wisdom of a modern Cleopatra, somehow succeeded in steering our book safely to harbour.

Finally, our profoundest thanks go to our (respective) wives, EJ and Fi, who have yet again endured so gracefully their husbands' lengthy journeys to antiquity and have supported us so graciously on our way. We could not have written this without them.

DS & SM 2012